THE TRAVEL SECRET

HOW TO PLAN YOUR BIG TRIP AND SEE THE WORLD

Sarah Kerrigan

Published by Goldcrest Books International Ltd
www.goldcrestbooks.com
publish@goldcrestbooks.com

ISBN: 978-1-911505-38-9
eISBN: 978-1-911505-39-6

In loving memory of Stephen Chapple

CONTENTS

INTRODUCTION

It was during my second round-the-world trip that I came up with the idea for this book. I was thinking about how, when I announced to my friends and colleagues that I was about to quit my job and take seven months off to travel in Australia, Southeast Asia and Central America, so many people said to me, *"you're so lucky,"* or *"I wish I could do that."*

But I'm not really that lucky and I want to show you how, with a little planning, you can do it too.

I'm a London-based, career-focussed professional keen to strike that ever-elusive work/life balance whilst continuing to climb the career ladder. I want to show you how you can balance taking time out to travel the world, whilst still building your career, developing yourself and having lots of fun whilst you're at it!

My travels have taken me to some far-flung corners of the world: I've scaled Mount Kinabalu in Borneo and snorkelled with sharks and stingrays in Belize; I've wandered around the ancient temples of Angkor in

Cambodia and the Mayan ruins in Mexico; I've crossed the international date line on the way to the Cook Islands and trekked up a mountain with elephants in Thailand. I've bungee jumped my way around the world, explored jungles and cloud forests, scuba-dived some of the world's best dive sites and hung out with indigenous locals from around the globe. By changing my attitude towards how I travel, I've seen so much more of the world than I could ever hope to achieve with a few weeks of annual leave each year.

Whatever your personal situation, I hope you can use this book as a guide to facilitate your trip – or trips – of a lifetime when the time is right. It's all about the planning after all, not upping sticks and leaving tomorrow. I hope this book will plant a seed that one day will germinate and become plans for an extended trip and change the way you see travel forever. I'll share with you my inspiration, practicalities, top tips and resources to turn your dream trip into reality – and lots of useful advice for when you're on the road.

Enjoy!

Sarah Kerrigan in Wedge, Western Australia

EXCUSE-BUSTERS!

I'm assuming you've bought this book because you're intrigued by the possibility of long-term travel; you want to know how to make your big trip a reality but are not sure where to start, or if it's even feasible for you. Between juggling commitments at home and earning a living it can feel nigh on impossible to one day pack it all in and head off to exotic climes – despite being high up the list of life goals of many people. You might feel like there are so many reasons you can't go travelling that you're sure it's an impossibility.

You may also encounter other people trying to put you off, or tell you why they think long-term travel is a *bad* idea, so before we get into the details of planning, let's get the excuses out of the way: all the reasons you tell yourself that you can't go travelling and what to say to the naysayers...

I can't afford it

Yes, you can. Maybe you can't afford to go tomorrow, this year, or even next year, but assign a realistic timeframe and put by a sensible amount of money each month and you will eventually have enough saved up.

For a basic estimate, calculate the rough cost of your ideal trip that you'd like to go on in X years, divide by X to get your annual savings required, and then divide by twelve to figure out how much you need to save each month to make it happen. Get planning and as soon as you hit your savings target, get booking! I'll discuss some budgeting tips in more detail later.

Or, just save as much as you can. If life gets in the way and you have unexpected outgoings, keep saving and you will eventually get there! Every pound, dollar or euro you put into your travel savings account is one step closer to realising your trip, even if it takes a long time to get there. Don't give up or lose sight of your goal and you will one day make your big trip happen.

You need to have a vivid vision of the future to inspire and motivate you to save up. Change your computer wallpaper to a picture of an inspirational travel destination and stick up postcards of locations you'd love to visit in places where you'll see them often to keep your trip front of mind.

Saving up is the hard part. Once you're on the road, you may even find that living expenses are minimal and your money goes a long way, especially if you're used to living in an expensive city like London, New York, Hong Kong or Sydney and are travelling in countries with a much cheaper cost of living – like much of Southeast Asia and parts of Central America.

I don't have time

You don't have time to take out three, six, or twelve months? Well, as with the saving up, it's just a matter of priorities and planning for it. In the grand scheme of things, taking a few months out won't make much difference to the future.

Aside from a potential gap year opportunity after university, most people wait their whole working life, taking nothing but short holidays (as dictated by their company's annual leave policy) until they retire. With people now living longer and the retirement age being pushed back further and further with each generation, doesn't it make sense to build in some career breaks, or some extended time off? Don't wait your whole life to do something that you've always wanted to do – and that you could make happen much sooner!

In his book, **The 4-Hour Work Week** (https://amzn. to/2t9ARHC), Timothy Ferriss talks about taking *mini-retirements* – regular, meaningful breaks from work and the daily grind; interspersing your working life with periods of rejuvenation and adventure – for example, six months of working hard and earning money, followed by six months out of the rat-race, slowing down, travelling, broadening the mind and enriching your life. Rinse and repeat.

Regular escapes from the nine-to-five give you an opportunity to revive yourself and refocus; to take time out to clarify your goals and enrich your life through adventure, away from the frenzied pace of modern life.

Why wait until you're nearly seventy to retire and take the opportunity to travel? Seize the day and plan some much-deserved time off now! Whilst life expectancy is going up, not everyone will be fortunate enough to live a long, healthy life. It's a paradox; make future plans assuming you will live well into old age, but try to enjoy life as if it's your last few months left on Earth.

Rolf Potts, travel guru and author of best-seller travel book **Vagabonding** (https://amzn.to/2teUoqa) asserts that time, not money, is true wealth. He says:

> *"Money, of course, is still needed to survive, but time is what you need to live. So, save what little money you possess to meet basic survival requirements, but spend your time lavishly in order to create the life values that make the fire worth the candle."*

> (Rolf Potts, *Vagabonding: An Uncommon Guide to the Art of Long-Term World Travel*, 1st edition, Villard Books 2003)

We live in a society where wealth is a status symbol; our success is judged on what possessions we own, the salary we earn and how we conform to this modern, consumerist idea of success. However, what's the point in having large sums of money if you have no time to spend them? Working long hours, evenings and weekends to earn a large salary is pointless if you have no time to enjoy the money you have earned.

Experiences create memories far more precious than expensive belongings, yet we still crave wealth and all its trimmings. We all need money to survive, but look beyond possessions for a richer, happier life.

For some food for thought and to kick start your wanderlust, watch this inspiring talk by Rolf Potts: Time = Wealth https://youtu.be/MFrhIdwpWx0 recorded for The DO Lectures (www.thedolectures.com).

I'm afraid to leave my job

Giving up a stable job and a regular income can be a big risk to take. Only you can make the call – but I've done it twice now and never looked back – and I plan to do it again!

The first time I went travelling I left my job, which I loved, but I wanted to travel more than I wanted to stay in that role, or with that company. I asked for a sabbatical, but they were unable to keep my job open for me, so I decided to resign and look for a new job when I came back from my travels.

Having budgeted some money to support myself during my job search when I got back home, I was no worse off financially – and I ultimately ended up in a better paying job, so the risk paid off.

Alternatively, could you ask your current company for a secondment overseas, take a job abroad, work remotely or volunteer whilst you travel to enable your newfound nomadic lifestyle?

Taking some time out permitted me to expand my horizons; take stock and refocus; to evaluate what I want from my career and tailor my job search to my situation and future wants. When we've been in a job for a few years, how many of us really take the opportunity to step back and re-evaluate where we're going and what we want from our careers? Travel really opened my eyes to this and it's hard to get this kind of perspective without stepping out of the rat race.

I've got kids

Okay, I know you can't take your children out of school without being penalised – plus you might lose your child's place in the class – so at first sight, that would leave you with the option of doing a shorter break over the summer holidays or waiting until they're older and take them with you (or leave them behind if they're much older and have flown the nest!)

This is where timeframe planning comes in. On my travels, I have seen plenty of parents travelling with children – yes, some of them may just be on holiday, but equally there are the ones who take the kids along for the travel experience. The wealth of life experience and the breadth of history and culture experienced on the road can be far more enriching and educating than any classroom environment.

Think outside of the box and figure out if there's a solution that might work for you. Can you home school your children whilst you travel? Think about how you can enrich their learning experience – teach them about geography and geology by seeing glaciers and volcanoes up close; practise languages by travelling in countries where that language is spoken; and count pebbles on the beach for maths lesson. Could you enrol them in an international school abroad and travel around that region during the school holidays?

Search the internet for family travel blogs and books for inspiration and tips on how to make your trip a reality. Lonely Planet's **Travel with Children: The Essential Guide for Travelling Families** (https:// amzn.to/2tcLgSZ) contains great advice and ideas for travelling as a family, including suggested destinations and practical itineraries, tips on healthy travel, travelling with teenagers and much more.

I don't have anyone to go with

It might sound scary or bold, but have you thought about travelling alone? You may be surprised to find that there are plenty of solo travellers out there, who actively want to go it alone and find individual travel to be a valuable and rewarding experience.

The benefits of solo travel are never having to ask someone where they want to go or what they want to do or eat, or waiting to synchronise schedules – you can be your own boss and are accountable to no one! Sure, if you travel with someone, you can agree to do your own thing and go your own separate ways if desired, but you might feel like you're letting them down, or disagree about the itinerary, so sometimes it's just easier to travel alone from the start.

Whilst it might initially seem intimidating, being forced out of your comfort zone is a great confidence builder, making you more likely to make conversation with new people and make new friends. (When travelling with a friend or partner you tend to chat only to them and can appear less approachable to other people.) You'll get to know yourself better and even open yourself up to some experiences that you might not have had when travelling with a friend.

It's important to remember that not all travellers are eighteen-year-old gap year students and during my time on the road, there were as many thirty- or forty-something-year-olds (and even retirees) as there were young backpackers.

Many of the backpacker routes are well-beaten paths and are popular for a reason – they are easy to travel, well connected, cover the best sights and places to visit and are often suitable for the budget-conscious traveller. You'll likely meet people doing the same route as you even if you start out on your own.

Travellers are, by and large, open-minded and sociable folk, who enjoy meeting other people and getting to know other cultures, so you'll by no means be alone. Sign up for tours and buddy up with people, opt for accommodation with a communal kitchen and lounge areas and get chatting to other guests. If you see other travellers on their own, ask if they fancy joining you to visit an attraction, do a tour or go out for dinner – the chances are they are in a similar position to you and may also love the company.

For an authentic local experience, can you stay with a local family? Check out **Airbnb** (www.airbnb.co.uk) or **Couchsurfing** (www.couchsurfing.com) listings for accommodation options in shared houses. Airbnb is great if you like your own space, but Couchsurfing is a better way to meet people with the added bonus of a free place to stay! Sign up to Airbnb using the following link and get £25 off your first trip (when spending £55 or more): https://abnb.me/e/hQ5iQ3zuNN.

Lonely Planet's **Solo Travel Handbook** (https://amzn. to/2taHVE4) is a great resource if you're thinking about planning a solo trip. It's full of tips and recommendations for how to beat the nerves and give you the confidence to go out and see the world on your own.

If solo travel really isn't for you, do you have a friend that has always wanted to travel? What about any old pacts with school friends to backpack around the world one day? Perhaps you could visit friends or family abroad as part of your trip, or have friends come along with you for sections of your wider trip?

I have caring duties at home

This is a trickier commitment to *'get out of'* – and not one that you would necessarily want to shirk – when it comes to caring for elderly relatives, loved-ones or even pets.

Consider if someone could cover your duties whilst you undertake a short trip – could a friend, family member, or even a professional carer could help out in the short term? Alternatively, could you plan your trip further into the future, when you might be able to get some assistance, or if you're likely to be less hands-on with caring?

Everyone is entitled to a break – caring full-time is tough and you need to make sure you look after yourself enough to ensure you can continue to offer the best care for your loved-ones. I'm not suggesting you abandon your duties entirely and leave the country to go travelling for a year, but a well-planned, shorter trip could fortify you for more dedicated care in the coming months.

It's never going to be the perfect time to travel and you'll always find a reason not to go – whether it's commitments at home, career aspirations you don't want to give up on or family and friends that you don't want to leave. But if you have always wanted to travel, make it happen sooner rather than later – I promise you won't regret it!

Now you've overcome the main excuses, let's get on with planning your big trip!

RESOURCES RECAP:

- The 4-Hour Work Week – Timothy Ferriss
  https://amzn.to/2t9ARHC

- Vagabonding: An Uncommon Guide to the Art of Long-Term World Travel – Rolf Potts
  https://amzn.to/2teUoqa

- The DO Lectures: (www.thedolectures.com)
  Time = Wealth https://youtu.be/MFrhIdwpWx0

- Travel with Children: The Essential Guide for Travelling Families – Lonely Planet
  https://amzn.to/2tcLgSZ

- Airbnb www.airbnb.co.uk. Sign up using the following link and get £25 off your first trip (when spending £55 or more)
  https://abnb.me/e/hQ5iQ3zuNN

- Couch surfing: www.couchsurfing.com

- The Solo Travel Handbook – Lonely Planet
  https://amzn.to/2taHVE4

2

WANDERLUST

To pique your wanderlust before you start planning your trip, here are some of my top travel experiences for inspiration. There's something here to suit all budgets including some free activities.

- **Learning to scuba dive in Sipadan, Borneo.** If you've always wanted to try scuba diving, then where better to learn than in one of the world's top dive sites. Channel your inner Jacques Cousteau, swim amongst giant sea turtles and marvel at huge coral walls whilst getting certified. It certainly beats learning in a swimming pool back home! I was amazed to see an enormous turtle on my first ever dive – and the diversity of sea life on display soon distracted me from my beginner's nerves. I learnt with Scuba Junkie (www.scuba-junkie.com, who come highly recommended). The course runs over three days and covers all the theory, study materials and practical experience you'll need to qualify for your PADI Open Water certificate.

Discovering the underwater world.

- **Soaking in the hot springs in La Fortuna, Costa Rica.** In the shadow of Costa Rica's Arenal volcano, soak and delight in the area's proliferation of natural hot springs. My favourite experience was wallowing in the flowing waters of a hot spring river. Part of the natural, undeveloped landscape, it's the reason why locals and tourists alike descend on the river – which is geothermally heated to thirty-eight degrees Celsius – and soothe tired muscles after a day's hiking in the tropical cloud forest.

Arenal volcano, Costa Rica.

- **Wine tasting in Marlborough, New Zealand.**
  Sign up to a tour, jump in a minivan and get driven
  around some of New Zealand's best wineries
  – from small-scale boutique vineyards to the
  producers of the global household wine brands we
  know and love – a wine tour is a fascinating insight
  into how my favourite tipple is made, with plenty
  of tasters throughout the day and the opportunity
  to buy direct from the cellar door. What's not to
  love?

Grapes ripening on the vine
Marlborough, New Zealand.

- **Swimming in the cenotes of Mexico's Yucatan Peninsula.** Cenotes are cool, fresh water pools formed in a collapsed limestone cave system and are a delightfully refreshing way to cool off. The water is so clear, which makes for excellent snorkelling and cave diving. There are around 6,000 cenotes dotted all over the Yucatan Peninsula – some are little more than pools in someone's back garden, while others have been developed into theme park style attractions. Whatever your preference, they are a must-see part of Mexico's landscape.

Gran Cenote – Yucatan Peninsula, Mexico.

- **Hiking up Mount Kinabalu in Malaysian Borneo.** A relatively easy hike in trekking terms, but a richly rewarding one. With a personal guide, I hiked to the base camp at three thousand metres on the afternoon of day one, refuelled and slept overnight at the hostel, rising in the early hours the following morning to hike to the summit in time to watch the sun come up. As you climb, watch the tropical climate and foliage at the foot of the mountain, turn into a barren, almost lunar landscape at the top; the temperature dropping as you climb, to a bitter wind chill at the 4,095-metre peak.

  Visit www.mountkinabalu.com for more information.

On top of the world! – Mount Kinabalu,
Malaysian Borneo.

- **Chilling out on Muri Beach, Rarotonga, Cook Islands.** Arguably the most beautiful spot on Rarotonga, Muri beach is set apart from the waves on the reef by a tranquil blue lagoon and *motu* (islets). I felt a million miles from anywhere in the remote Cook Islands, experiencing island lifestyle at its best! I whiled away my days reading on the beach, snorkelling in the lagoon, learning twenty different ways to tie a sarong, how to crack open a coconut and watching impressive live drumming and dance performances.

Muri Lagoon – Rarotonga, Cook Islands.

- **Eating tapas in Barcelona, Spain.** It's always a pleasure to visit countries and regions famed for their regional produce and culinary skills, and Cataluña is no exception. From simple, rustic and local dishes to fine dining, Catalan cuisine is amongst the best in the world. There's excellent local seafood, hot and spicy *patatas bravas*, cured meats, the famous 'pan de tomat' (*tomato bread*) and excellent regional wines; a tapas dinner delights the senses – especially when eaten alfresco on a summer's evening, with views out over the city or the ocean.

Tapas – Barcelona, Spain

- **Having a mud spa with happy elephants in Chiang Mai, Thailand.** I had an absolute ball at Dumbo Elephant Spa. (http://dumboelephantspa.com) After spending the morning feeding the elephants their breakfast then hiking with them up a mountain, we donned our swimwear and wallowed with the elephants in a big muddy pool, slinging mud at them – much to their delight. The noise made by a happy elephant is very different to the trumpeting sound you'd normally associate with an elephant! Once everyone was covered head to toe in mud (us included), we walked down to a nearby river to wash it all off – though I'm not sure I'll ever get all the mud out of my bikini! What a charming and ethical way to get up close and personal with these gentle giants in their natural environment.

Hanging out with the elephants at Dumbo Elephant Spa – Chiang Mai, Thailand.

- **Walking on the lava fields on Mount Etna, Sicily, Italy.** Experience the thrill of hiking on this still active volcano, in sight of the *smoking* cone. Temperatures are cooler at the altitude of the volcano, making for a pleasant escape from the summer heat and humidity at sea level. In a small group we trekked along footpaths to stunning viewpoints over the volcano, before going off-piste and running down through the black sand to get back down to the bottom – a bit like running down a giant sand dune. We were shaking volcanic sand and ash out of our shoes for ages after that hike! Go with a guide for the best experience.

Mount Etna, Sicily, Italy.

- **Drinking coffee in Colombia.** Drinking coffee in a coffee producing country really gives you a different perspective on your morning caffeine fix. Of all the coffee-producing places I have visited, I think Colombian coffee is my favourite – and the ritual of drinking it becomes more than grabbing a quick cup on your way out. I loved taking the time to understand more about how it's produced and the journey from bean to cup and I never knew what a fresh coffee bean looked like before it makes its way to somewhere like Starbucks!

I was fascinated to discover that the richness of flavour is inversely proportionate to the amount of caffeine in a cup – so what tastes like a weak brew actually has more caffeine than a dark, rich and strong-tasting cup – and therefore espresso is one of the weaker drinks when it comes to getting your caffeine hit!

Enjoying coffee in Colombia.

- **Descend into the underworld and visit the catacombs in Paris, France.** One of Paris's lesser-known attractions, and with a gory history to boot, the catacombs were constructed in the late eighteenth century and contain the bones of over six million people, in a bid to deal with the overcrowding and subsequent exhuming of Parisian cemeteries. What began as a disorderly pile of bones, soon became the decorative organisation of skulls and femurs into patterns, creating a mausoleum that people could visit to pay their respects. These creative displays of bones can still be seen today. Visiting is certainly not a *scary* experience, though perhaps a little creepy – we spoke to the guards who work there, who said despite spending every day there, they never liked to be down there alone. I guess when a place is steeped in so much history, even the most pragmatic person might be fearful of ghosts! It's definitely worth a visit if you find yourself in Paris. Visit http://www.catacombes.paris.fr for more details.

The Catacombs – Paris, France

- **Watching the sun rise over Angkor Wat, Cambodia.** Stand in awe and watch as the huge temple emerges at dawn as the sun comes up. If the weather is good, you'll get impressive views of the temple with the sunrise as your backdrop, but even if it's overcast (as it was when I was there), you'll still be bowled over by the grandeur, the striking architecture, intricate details, and the imposing history of this lost culture and civilisation. Whether you're an avid history buff, or casual holidaymaker, you can't fail to be impressed by the temples of Angkor. From your first sight of Angkor Wat, head into the jungle to see the *'Tomb Raider'* temple overgrown amongst twisted tree roots; followed by the two hundred faces that are carved into the towers of Bayon temple, it really has to be seen to be believed.

Bayon Temple – Angkor Wat, Cambodia

- **Watching a live 'banda' performance in Oaxaca, Mexico.** Think you've heard brass bands? Think again and listen to this energetic and colourful Mexican interpretation! In the Zocalo, Oaxaca's central square there's nightly entertainment – the best of which is the *'banda'* music. The band, made up predominantly of brass, clarinets and percussion, performs lively, soulful and happy music that cannot fail to make you feel alive. There's a real pride amongst the performers as they sing and play their hearts out. Be sure to seek this out for an authentic, inspiring and joyful Mexican experience.

I also love the Mariachi bands heard across Mexico, who play with a similar joy and passion!

Mariachi band – Tulum, Mexico.

- **Thai massage on the Khaosan Road, Bangkok, Thailand.** You don't have to look far in Thailand to find a decent Thai massage, but I think **K Massage**, just off Bangkok's infamous Khaosan Road, was probably my favourite establishment and I enjoyed a lot of great treatments here. I loved watching the world go by with a foot rub on a chair outside on the terrace; or a full body massage in the warren of treatment rooms inside. Always a thorough, strong and rigorous treatment, it was perfect for ironing out the aches and pains of carrying around my heavy rucksack – and I couldn't get enough of it!

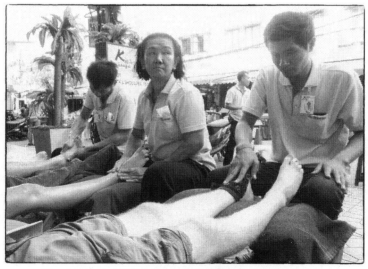

Footrub at K Massage – Bangkok, Thailand.

- **Bungee jumping off the Verzasca Dam, Locarno, Switzerland.** I've clocked up a fair number of bungee jumps around the world, but the **007 GoldenEye jump** has to be my favourite! The jump is named after the film of the same name, where James Bond leaps off the dam in the opening sequence of the film. The jump consists of a 220-metre leap and is not for the faint hearted! As I queued up to jump (yes, there is a queue!) I watched the two people ahead of me *chicken out.* It is probably the most exhilarating jump I've done and I definitely want to go back and do it again!

Visit www.trekking.ch/en/bungy/007-bungy-jumping-verzasca-like-james-bond for more details and to book your jump.

Bungee jump like James Bond! Verzasca Dam, Locarno, Switzerland

- **Watching the waves in Zipolite, on Mexico's Pacific Coast.** I could sit and watch the waves pound the shore all day in Zipolite, as enormous rollers crash dramatically into the bay from across the Pacific. The power of the water as it is thrown down with an almighty splash onto the shore is always impressive and there is no shortage of beachside bars and restaurants from which you can take in the view. The only downside, of course, is that the waves are so big and the currents so strong, that you're not allowed to swim – but not even the best swimmer in the world would want to take on those waves if they were in their right mind! If you're desperate for a dip, head along the coast for a few minutes to Mazunte, where it's safe to swim, but caution is advised as the currents are still strong and the waves can knock you off your feet. I loved watching the boats race to shore in between the breakers in the perfect combination of speed and timing!

Zipolite, Mexico.

- **Quad biking in Kalbarri national park, Western Australia.** What sets this apart from other quad biking tours is the absolutely stunning setting on Wagoe Beach in Kalbarri National Park. We watched huge waves spray up into the air as they hit the reef just off-shore, as we sped along the beach and over sand dunes on our quad bikes. The views were sensational, and our group had the entire beach to ourselves. This is Australia's huge-scale natural beauty at its best, with an adrenaline boost to boot!

  Visit www.kalbarriquad.com for further information.

Quad-biking on Wagoe Beach –
Kalbarri National Park, Australia.

- **Learning to cook Thai food in Chaing Rai, Thailand.** Learning to cook traditional Thai dishes with chef Suwanee was a fun and informative experience. It included a visit to the market to buy supplies, an education on Thai cooking and ingredients, and the opportunity to sample loads of local delicacies. On the way to the market, we agreed as a group what dishes we'd like to learn to cook and settled on hot and sour prawn soup (*tom yum kung*), Thai red curry with chicken (*keng ped gai*), pad Thai with chicken and bananas in coconut milk (*kluay buat chee*) for dessert – then went back to the house to make them. We rounded off the day by sitting down to eat all the food we'd prepared and it was delicious! We left with the recipes and photos of each stage in the cooking and preparation process, with every intention of making them another time. Find out more about Suwanee and book a class here: www. thaicookingclasschiangrai.com

"Tom yum kung" – Chiang Rai, Thailand.

- **Walking the coastal paths in West Cornwall.**
This is technically not travel for me as it's where I
grew up, but Cornwall has some of the world's best
beaches and the high granite cliffs, golden sandy
beaches and turquoise waters are breath-taking!
I love to go out for long walks on the cliffs and
beaches when I go home. You can't beat Cornwall
when the weather is good – sadly, though, coastal
fog and rain are all too familiar! Be sure to check
out **Porthcurno** with the picturesque **Minack
Theatre** (www.minack.com) carved into the cliff,
looking out over Pedn Vounder Beach and the
Logan Rock for one of my favourite views in all
the world!

Porthcurno Beach – Cornwall, UK.

RESOURCES RECAP:

- **Scuba Junkie** www.scuba-junkie.com
- **Mount Kinabalu Climb Information & Booking Centre** www.mountkinabalu.com
- **Dumbo Elephant Spa** http://dumboelephantspa.com
- **Paris Catacombs** http://www.catacombes.paris.fr
- **007 GoldenEye bungee jump** www.trekking.ch/en/bungy/007-bungy-jumping-verzasca-like-james-bond
- **Kalbarri Wagoe Beach Quad Bike Tours** www.kalbarriquad.com
- **Suwannee Thai Cooking Class Chiangrai** www.thaicookingclasschiangrai.com
- **Minack Theatre** www.minack.com

3

HOW TO PLAN A CAREER BREAK

Taking a career break is easier than you might think and once you've set your mind on it, the process is a simple but meticulous matter of planning, with a clear end goal in sight. I'll talk you through some of the steps you need to take to set the ball rolling.

Budgeting and saving up

First things first, you need to figure out the basic cost of your trip – and it can be a very rough estimate at this stage. Start by asking yourself the following questions:

- *How long would I like to go away for?*
- *What are my monthly expenses?*

Multiply these together and this will give you a ballpark budget for your trip.

To calculate your monthly expenses, you'll need to factor in your living expenses at home and the costs associated with keeping your household going (mortgage or rent, water, gas, electricity, council tax, phone, broadband,

TV and so on) or the associated costs with renting or subletting your property, if applicable. Be sure to check with your lender or landlord the ramifications of having tenants if you're thinking about subletting!

Once you know how much it costs to keep your home going, you'll need a rough estimate of your monthly expenditure on the trip. This is a bit like asking *"how long is a piece of string?"* as it really depends on where you're planning on going and how luxuriously you hope to live when you're travelling. I'd recommend picking up travel guide books for the countries you're thinking about visiting or set the ball rolling with a quick Google search. **Lonely Planet** (www.lonelyplanet.com) and **Rough Guide** (www.roughguides.com) are two of the most popular – both of which include approximate costings per country – and take it from there. For your budget's sake, it's also worth making your itinerary a mix of cheaper and more expensive countries – you'll be amazed how far your money will go somewhere like Cambodia, versus Australia.

Next, factor in preferences like whether you'll be staying in private rooms in guesthouses, four- or five-star hotels, or the most budget-friendly option of a bed in a hostel dormitory. In some Caribbean locations, you have the even cheaper option of renting a hammock with a mosquito net on the beach!

Also, consider if you will be cooking all of your meals versus eating all of your meals out? Will you take internal flights and taxis everywhere or long-distance buses and public transport? When you're not confined to a short holiday, you have time to take a slower form of transport – whether it's to save money, or to enjoy the scenic route. It can be a mixture of the above, of course, tailored to the countries you're travelling in and you can easily check rough prices online in advance to help you refine your budget.

Lastly, think about how long you'd like to be away for and multiply it by your monthly estimate. Add in the rough cost of your flights and you'll have an estimate for the whole trip. Once you've calculated your budget, it's prudent to add a little – think of it as a buffer in case you're hit with some unexpected expenses or just want to extend your trip.

Now for the hardest part – saving up the amount you've calculated above.

Perhaps you have a fixed future date in mind for your trip, or maybe you'll just plan to go away when you hit your target amount in your savings account – either is fine but you need to be disciplined when it comes to saving up.

Unless you've just won the lottery or someone else is going to pay (I wish!), the chances are you'll need to make sacrifices in order to save up – whether it's making your own morning coffee instead of buying it in a coffee shop; cooking more and eating out less, reducing your monthly clothes shopping budget, taking in a lodger, or getting a second job to help save up, it all adds up over time and the steps you take will reflect your saving timeline.

Tracking your spending is key to identifying areas where you can cut back and to monitor whether your saving is on track. Keep a note of everything you purchase and analyse your credit card and bank statements lest you begin to slip back into old habits.

It may sound obvious but, whilst you're saving up, try to stop buying more stuff – including (to a degree) buying things to take travelling with you – and start getting rid of anything that might tie to you to your current location. Pay off any debt, clear out your possessions, declutter and get used to living more minimally – it will be good practice for when you're on the road and all your worldly possessions will need to fit into a bag on your back. If you need travel gear, could you consider picking up second hand guide books and essentials to save money?

Saving is not meant to be easy or fun, however there seems to be a positive correlation between the effort required to make the trip happen and the benefit gained from the travels. That is to say the travellers who have spent many months or years meticulously saving hard and planning their *big trip* are most richly rewarded by the experience. Contrast this with those referred to as *"trustafarians"*- travelling the world on someone else's money, with no real plan; flip-flopping from one place to the next without any real purpose, goal or end date in sight.

Rolf Potts writes:

> *"Ironically, the best litmus test for measuring your vagabonding gumption is found not in travel but in the process of earning your freedom to travel. Earning your freedom, of course, involves work—and work is intrinsic to vagabonding for psychic reasons as much as financial ones. To see the psychic importance of work, one need look no further than people who travel the world on family money. Sometimes referred to as "trustafarians," these folks are among*

the most visible and least happy wanderers in the travel milieu. Draping themselves in local fashions, they flit from one exotic travel scene to another, compulsively volunteering in local political causes, experimenting with exotic intoxicants, and dabbling in every non-Western religion imaginable. Talk to them, and they'll tell you they're searching for something "meaningful."

... What they're really looking for, however, is the reason why they started traveling in the first place. Because they never worked for their freedom, their travel experiences have no personal reference— no connection to the rest of their lives. They are spending plenty of time and money on the road, but they never spent enough of themselves to begin with. Thus, their experience of travel has a diminished sense of value."

(Rolf Potts, *Vagabonding: An Uncommon Guide to the Art of Long-Term World Travel,* 1st edition, Villard Books 2003)

Don't think you need to be earning big bucks to make an extended trip a reality – on my first trip, I was only a few years into my career and I was not on a high salary. Give yourself the time to save regularly and you will slowly get there – this may seem obvious, or patronising but saving requires serious discipline. Use the end goal as fire in your belly to motivate you to save for your upcoming trip and you may be surprised at how much you can put away when you really put your mind to it.

For both of my trips, I saved up gradually, over a number of years, in between organising and paying for a wedding, moving house, buying a flat and going on a few holidays. It was slow progress at times, but I put away as much as I could afford each month (which was sometimes nothing!) As I approached my target budget, I started planning the trip in more detail until I was able to set a departure date and make a solid plan.

Work commitments

The need for discretion

This is a tricky one. You've decided to start planning the trip of a lifetime – but your departure might be one, two or five years away. Even when you're counting down the final six months, the chances are your notice period in your job is one to three months, so you don't want to tell anyone too soon – your employer might not take too kindly to the fact you're planning on leaving and you don't want to be overlooked for promotion in the meantime – so, be discreet about who you tell.

It killed me to keep my trips such a secret – I considered my colleagues to be my friends and I was dying to share my excitement with them, but I was also saving up over a long timeframe so even though I knew I would eventually travel, I didn't tell anyone until I handed in my one month's notice.

After completing my first round-the-world trip, I remember coming home and looking for a new job. In the interviews, I was asked about my travels and I talked about how much I enjoyed them – but I also said that ultimately, I was ready to settle down and focus on my career now. This was true in part, but I also couldn't wait to start saving up to do it all again! Long-term travel had awakened in me a desire to travel more, not less – but I had to play it down. After all, I could hardly go into an interview, or start a new job saying, *"by the way I might leave in five years to travel again!"* – even if it is true!

So, by all means, tell your family and dearest friends – they can help keep your saving on track and keep you motivated – but watch out for letting too much slip to the wrong people, especially if they can't keep a secret.

Working remotely

Depending on your line of work and the flexibility of your employer, you may be able to work remotely from around the world. Consider the nature of your job, the equipment you need and whether it would be possible to do it in a remote location and across different time zones.

If you're staying somewhere longer-term, you could think about renting an apartment, or a hotel with a decent amount of space and a desk. You don't want to be sitting on your bed in a hostel trying to conduct a **Skype** (www.skype.com) call or hurt your back from hunching over a laptop screen.

Bear in mind where your clients or customers are based and whether you need to be available for them over the phone or in person. If your clients are in the United Kingdom but you are travelling in Australia you will be on opposite time zones so make sure you agree in advance your working arrangements, deadlines and when you will be available to contact.

Time zones can also work in your favour, however. Say your employer or clients are based in the UK and you are travelling in Mexico. They can hand over assignments at the end of their working day, which you work on during your day whilst they are at home asleep – and then deliver it to them by the time they come into the office on the following morning.

I set up my own Virtual Assistant business, **Admin Land** (www.admin.land), to enable me to work and earn remotely whilst I travel. This plays on my strengths and background as a Personal Assistant. The nature of the job also makes it possible to work from anywhere – all I need is a laptop and an internet connection. Think about what might work for you in your field.

Working by the pool in Tulum, Mexico.

The trend for **digital nomads** around the world is growing, and cities like Chiang Mai and Bangkok, Thailand, Ho Chi Minh City, Vietnam, Ubud (Bali), Indonesia and Barcelona, Spain are getting a reputation for being some of the best places to live cheaply and work remotely with a laptop over Wi-Fi.

Working whilst travelling does throw up some challenges, however, so make sure you're prepared. You need to decide how you'll fit the travel around your work. Do you plan to stay in one place for a while? Do you need to work fixed hours each day (for example to correspond with the time zone of your clients' or employer's head office)? Of course, the plus side to working remotely is that your travels will be a lot more sustainable as you'll be earning money as you go, so you can be more flexible with your return date, if you wish.

Younger travellers can apply for a working holiday visa (upper age limits vary per country) and pick up bar work, or fruit picking jobs along the way. It tends to be low paid work but on the plus side, there's plenty of it (especially in peak season); picking up short-term, casual work in each town along the way is a great way to fund your travels, plus it's sociable and a good way to meet other travellers.

The search for fast Wi-Fi can plague your travels, especially if you're used to a super-fast connection at home. Consider working from co-working spaces if you need a guaranteed internet speed or be prepared to have a back-up plan if the Wi-Fi connection fails you and you can't get online.

You can usually bed in for an hour or two at a coffee shop, paying your rent in coffee in exchange for the WI-FI password and (if you're lucky) a plug socket. If you regularly work from coffee shops, you'll become an expert in stretching that coffee out for two hours whilst your devices charge up and you get on top of your emails!

WiFiMap (www.wifimap.io) is a useful app which contains over one hundred million accessible Wi-Fi hotspot locations. It is a user-updated database, detailing hundreds of nearby Wi-Fi passwords. Wherever you are in the world, simply open the app to access the passwords of nearby networks. When you've connected to a new network, you can also update the database for other users. The only catch is that you need to be online to connect and download the database. Upgrade to the pro version for a one-off nominal charge to be able to download an entire city's Wi-Fi passwords before you get there and access them offline when you arrive.

It's really useful to have some data on your phone (consider unlocking your phone before you go and get a local SIM card) or even get an Internet dongle when you arrive so you have a back-up method for getting online if the Wi-Fi is slow or non-existent.

Check to see if your current mobile tariff includes roaming in the countries you plan on visiting, and any associated costs. For example, roaming charges in the European Union have now been dropped by network providers in those countries, however, always check the small print before going online to avoid any unexpected expensive monthly bills.

Speedtest.net (www.speedtest.net) is an invaluable resource on the road: a website which enables you to run an internet speed test – testing upload and download speeds in a short thirty-second test.

On my recent travels, if I knew I had work to do or calls to make and needed a fast connection, I would ask the host to run the test remotely before booking online or do it in person on arrival – before handing over the money for the accommodation.

The **SimpleSpeed** app for iPhone offers the same functionality in an app for convenience on the go.

Taking a sabbatical

Depending on the Human Resources policies of the company you work for, it is worth asking your line manager if it's possible to take an unpaid sabbatical as, unless you're desperate to leave your job, a sabbatical would give you the peace of mind that you have a job to return to when you come home.

My advice on asking your boss for a sabbatical would be to have a hypothetical conversation with him or her. Try not to make it sound like a threat (*"if you don't give me a sabbatical I'm leaving anyway!"*) and ask, *"if I were to consider taking some time out, would it be possible for the company to offer me an unpaid sabbatical?"*

It's likely your boss's ears will prick up at this point! If the hypothetical conversation goes well, go in with your proposed length of trip and approximate departure date and ask if they could check with Human Resources and find out your next steps.

If a sabbatical is not possible – which it wasn't in my case (for either trip) – at least you've explored that option and know where you stand. Leave on good terms and you can apply for any suitable open positions at the same company when you return or use your departure as an excuse to go for a job with more money or increased responsibility with a new organisation.

Check out this great **TED** talk by Stefan Sagmeister on **The Power Of Time Off**, which looks at the benefits of a sabbatical to break up work and renew creativity: www.ted.com/talks/stefan_sagmeister_the_power_of_time_off

Volunteering

Don't let your skills atrophy or go to waste on a career break. You may have swapped the office for the open road, but you can combine your time away, skills and expertise to do good by volunteering or working in community and charity projects in your chosen destination. What is more, volunteering and charity work is great work experience and looks good on your CV, especially if it's relevant to your profession or a cause that's close to your heart.

Whether you are volunteering in a formal organisation, or offering to help out in a local community, consider what skills you have that you can offer. It could be language skills, teaching, medical aid or legal advice.

For many charities, the best help you can give them is to raise funds and awareness for their cause. Volunteering your time for any given charity is not always an option –

especially if specialist knowledge or skills are required. Consider how much further your money could go by giving it to trained experts, versus them using the funds to train you up.

With a little research you'll find lots of projects you can get involved in. Here are some of the most popular organisations and a great place to begin your search.

World Wide Opportunities on Organic Farms (WWOOF)

WWOOF (http://wwoof.net) connects volunteers with organic farmers and growers in over fifty countries worldwide. As a volunteer (or WWOOFer) you will live alongside your host helping with daily tasks and experiencing life as a farmer. No prior farming experience is required. You'll be expected to do around four to six hours of work per day in return for a day's accommodation and food.

Once a member, you can search for opportunities by country, then contact a host farm to arrange your stay and discuss the type of volunteer work you'll be expected to do. You'll negotiate the length of your stay with your host prior to arrival – which could be anything from two days to six months, though the average placement tends to be around two to three weeks.

Some of the tasks you might be allocated are milking cows and feeding the animals; weeding, pruning or sowing seed; helping with the harvest; learning how to create mud bricks or build straw houses; preparing compost, cutting wood, growing vegetables, beekeeping, wine, bread and cheese making, and much more besides.

Before booking your first stay, think about the kind of experience you want to gain, including what skills you have to offer and what interests you most. Can you speak the language and is this necessary to get by?

Consider how long you want to work for and take your time to pick the right host – get to know them as much as you can before booking to ensure there's a rapport there and a mutual understanding of what's expected of you – you don't want to be tasked with milking the cows if you're not an *'animal person'*! Don't expect luxury accommodation or underestimate the hard work involved – farming requires a certain degree of physical fitness so try a shorter stay before committing to a long stint as a WWOOFer.

Lastly, as a volunteer, remember the work comes first so it's important that you don't let your host down. Go with an open mind, be prepared to get your hands dirty and have fun!

Teaching English as a Foreign Language (TEFL)

If you have a native or near-native level of English, you could teach English to help fund your travels.

TEFL (www.tefl.org.uk) believe that if you can speak English, you have the potential to teach it and no prior teaching experience is required. They offer a wide variety of online and classroom-based courses, covering the basics to more advanced and specialist modules to get you up to speed.

Once qualified, browse their website for teaching jobs including full-time, part-time and freelance opportunities in primary and secondary schools, universities, business schools, translation companies and summer schools. You will find residential options, and some even provide your flight, food and lodgings in addition to a salary.

If your English teaching qualification is not from TEFL. org.uk, check out the job opportunities on **TEFL.com** (www.tefl.com) and **Dave's ESL Café** (www.eslcafe. com)

Workaway

Workaway (www.workaway.info) believe that volunteering opportunities abroad need not be expensive (nor do they mean that you have to clean toilets day in day out – unless you want to, of course!)

Ideal for budget travellers, language students or culture vultures, Workaway help find work placements and volunteering opportunities in over 170 countries worldwide. In exchange for a few hours' work per day they will provide your meals and accommodation and you'll also be able to learn about the local lifestyle and community. It's a great way to give back to the community and stretch out your travel money.

From NGOs and schools, to farm stays and local families, the range of work and duties is broad and placements can be from as short as two weeks to much longer durations – simply negotiate the finer details with your host before you begin. As with WWOOFing, take the time to pick and get to know your host – there are so many options out there, so search for a good fit and rapport before committing and don't let them down.

You can register with Workaway from as little as USD $29 per year. Find out more about the available opportunities at www.workaway.info.

Conservation projects

Conservation projects working with animals such as orangutans in Borneo, elephants in Thailand or turtles in the Galapagos are popular and programmes are widespread, so do some research before you go to find the right one for you. A simple Google search should get the ball rolling, or you could ask locally when you arrive.

Choose your charity wisely; commit to help them and always carry out the work you have agreed to do for them. Your efforts go a long way to help a cause or community who rely on the efforts of volunteers, so don't let them down.

Travel responsibly and support local conservation, cultural and environmental projects wherever you go. Do your bit to understand the threats to the local environment or wildlife and avoid signing up for any tours that exploit or threaten the flora, fauna or culture.

I spent some time with elephants in Northern Thailand and it was important to me that I chose an organisation that didn't exploit, endanger or harm the animals. I did some research to understand the current threats to elephants and their environment, and how best to support them.

If tourists are better educated on how they can impact animal well-being, they can demand improved conditions for the animals and eliminate the demand for the exploitation of these beautiful giants. It astonishes me that in this day and age people still want to see animals doing tricks in circuses or ride on their backs when it hurts them...

Dumbo Elephant Spa – Chiang Mai, Thailand.

Pack For A Purpose

Pack For A Purpose is a great little initiative which enables charity projects to benefit from excess capacity in your luggage.

Before you travel, check Pack For A Purpose (www. packforapurpose.org) to see what community projects are being run in the area you're visiting, then fill any space in your bag with supplies and provisions required by the project.

Not decided where to go yet? Select the initiative you'd like to support (health, child welfare, education, animal welfare or socio-economic development) to see what projects are being run worldwide.

Once you've chosen your project, review the list of supplies needed and decide what you'd like to donate. The supplies requested are varied – pens and pencils, books, art supplies, first aid kits, gardening tools, baby milk formula, animal supplies, clothes and shoes... Perhaps it's something you have at home already and no longer need; it could be donations from your workplace, or low cost items you'd like to buy to support a project close to your heart.

Once you've arrived in your destination, simply drop off the provisions at an accommodation or tour company that supports the project, and they will deliver them to the project on your behalf.

Lend With Care

Another good way to help and support good causes in developing countries is to invest your money in **Lend**

With Care (www.lendwithcare.org), where you can loan an entrepreneur in the developing world a small sum of money, which they pay back to you when they've made the money back from their business. You can choose your entrepreneur based on their profile, or filter by location, business activity or gender. Loans start from as little as £15 and you can invest in as many or as few business ventures as you like.

You don't have to visit the country or region to be able to help and can even invest in a project from the comfort of your own home. However, it's also a great way to support a region that you have visited and continue to invest in it after you have moved on.

Your loan, however small, makes a huge difference to local entrepreneurs and getting your money repaid to you once they have the business success to pay it back gives you a warm glow inside.

Finding your feet when you get home

When you get back home after your travels, you'll need to quickly re-establish yourself and settle back into a routine, whether old and familiar, or a new start – it's up to you!

My best advice to you is to factor into your budget for a few months' expenditure to allow yourself to settle in when you arrive back home. This will give you time to find a job, whilst ensuring the bills can be paid and cover any unforeseen expenses that may arise. I tend to budget for an additional three months in savings, which is usually ample. You may choose to budget for more or less depending on your circumstances.

You might need to find a new place to live, reconnect utilities, get ready for the kids to go back to school, set up meetings and more. Make a list of everything you need to think about so nothing gets forgotten and you can quickly work your way through it on your return.

Dealing with the gap on your CV

To be honest, I've never had a problem explaining the gap on my CV when I've taken time out to travel. If anything, it's a point of interest and certainly not a negative. I took some advice from a friend who's an HR professional with a lot of recruitment experience; he advised it's best to explain any gaps of six-months or more – as recruiters are only going to ask the question anyway. I have chosen to put in a line to explain my two seven-month travel gaps and recruiters have never taken issue with my taking a career break.

There's certainly nothing to be ashamed of if you take some time out, and recruiters, employers and colleagues alike are all likely to be envious of your adventures! It demonstrates a desire to understand other cultures and broaden your horizons, which are desirable attributes for an employee in any international organisation. Never apologise to any recruiter for taking time out to travel! You have demonstrated a positive choice to go away and realise the trip of a lifetime, not to mention the skills you picked up along the way.

Your experience – whilst not acquired through employment – is still an added layer of skills and knowledge that work in your favour, so think about how you can bring the benefits of your time out to your new role. Communication and negotiation skills; being able to self-motivate and work independently; the ability to be flexible and improvise; complex travel and logistics planning are all skills you will utilise when undertaking long-term travel.

If you choose to volunteer or work abroad, think about how this experience will enhance your skills and CV. Also, be prepared to discuss why you are passionate about the charity or cause and how you were able to make a difference.

A month before I returned home from my travels, I updated my CV and started sending it out to recruitment agencies and potential employers, so I could start lining up interviews as soon as I got back. This really enabled me to hit the ground running, and maximise my time in terms of job hunting, and my savings in terms of how long I needed to live off them.

But that's enough about coming home for now – let's get on with the more exciting business of planning your big trip!

RESOURCES RECAP:

- **Rough Guide** www.roughguides.com
- **Lonely Planet** www.lonelyplanet.com
- **Vagabonding: An Uncommon Guide to the Art of Long-Term World Travel** – Rolf Potts https://amzn.to/2teUoqa
- **Skype** www.skype.com
- **Admin Land** www.admin.land
- **WiFiMap** www.wifimap.io
- **Speedtest.net** www.speedtest.net
- **TED** talk by Stefan Sagmeister: **The Power Of Time Off** www.ted.com/talks/stefan_sagmeister_the_ power_of_time_off
- **World Wide Opportunities on Organic Farms (WWOOF)** http://wwoof.net
- **Teaching English as a Foreign Language (TEFL)** www.tefl.org.uk
- **TEFL.com** www.tefl.com
- **Dave's ESL Café** www.eslcafe.com
- **Workaway** www.workaway.info
- **Pack for a Purpose** www.packforapurpose.org
- **Lend with care** www.lendwithcare.org

4

HOW TO PLAN YOUR TRIP

Where and when to go

One of the biggest decisions to make is where to go on your big trip. The world is your oyster, so get inspired and have a think about where you've always wanted to visit.

You can't see everywhere (well, not in one trip anyway!) but there are loads of classic routes and itineraries out there. A good tip is to plan broadly where you want to go (e.g. which countries and regions), but beyond that try not to over-plan, as you'll want to be able to have the freedom to stay longer in a place you love or move on if somewhere isn't as good as expected.

Three key things to factor in are the activities you enjoy doing, the weather and the cost of living, which I'll look at in more detail now.

What do you like to do?

Are you a beach bum, thrill-seeker, history buff – or a mixture of the above? I'd recommend you try to get a mixture of activities on your travels: breaking up a long trip with mini varied *holidays*, such as a week at beach location, followed by a cultural city break, then an adventure in the rainforest or mountains. Keep your itinerary exciting and vary your pace so you don't overdo it or get bored.

Guide books will help you get the ball rolling with proposed itineraries for different length trips and advice on the best time of year to travel, but once you've got a few ideas about destinations, look beyond the guide books to plan your trip. There are hundreds of resources online – from personal travel blogs, to regional tourist information websites and travel booking sites, so take some time to browse and build your ideal itinerary.

There's also loads of practical advice out there – detailed blogs about border crossings, forums discussing long-distance bus and train timetables, connections, where to go and what to avoid. You should be able to find the answer to pretty much any question online if you're prepared to search for it. For example, when I was unsure of the border procedure and onward bus times in Laos, a quick Google search brought up a detailed blog which included the full bus timetable, a detailed description of the journey and even photos of the sleeper bus I'd be travelling on!

Take guide books, advice and reviews with a pinch of salt, however, and try not to rely too heavily on them. Guide books are great for getting a feel for a country or region, finding things to do and the best areas to stay, but I have often found that establishments that have been highly rated in guide books, can sometimes become complacent and lose their charm. They have a guaranteed pipeline of customers willing to take the guide book at face value, so they don't have to work at getting and retaining customers – something I like to refer to as *"the guide book effect"*. Some travellers even go as far as *avoiding* anywhere reviewed in the guide book!

Longer-term travel is a great opportunity to visit those far-flung, or hard to get to places that you can't comfortably cover in one to two weeks' annual leave. When in a region, take the opportunity to hop over the border into neighbouring countries and explore the surrounding area.

At around three weeks into your extended trip, you'll experience a new state of relaxation as you see your trip unfolding before you into the future. You'll realise that there's only so much you can do and unwind when you're on your two weeks' annual leave – and the feeling that you haven't got to go back to work is awesome!

What's the weather like?

Weather and temperature vary wildly around the world, so the local climate is a big factor in when to go and what clothes to pack for your chosen destination. You don't want to turn up in your shorts and t-shirt expecting a sunny beach break, only to find that it's freezing cold, or worse, hurricane or monsoon season! I've always enjoyed coinciding my travels with the UK winter and going somewhere hot to escape the cold weather. Then I arrange to land back in London when it's summer again – that's a great feeling if you don't like the cold. You also save on the cost of heating your home all winter!

If you're thinking about heading to the tropics, research when rainy season and dry season fall in your chosen destinations and plan accordingly. Even countries within the same part of the world have their own microclimates and seasonal variations – and even within different regions of the same country too.

Temperatures and seasons vary more distinctly in temperate climates, so you may choose to avoid Southern Europe (e.g. Athens, Greece or Rome, Italy) in the summer when it's forty degrees Centigrade, or Northern Europe (e.g. Amsterdam, Netherlands or Paris, France) in winter when temperatures can hit freezing, and instead favour travelling in spring or autumn.

The Best Time To Visit website (www.thebesttimetovisit. com) is a great resource to discover the best places to visit by month, season, or region. Search according to your own minimum and maximum temperature preferences, to help decide where to go.

Consider if it's peak, off-peak or *shoulder* season: peak season may appeal if you want the best weather and popular travel dates, but it will also mean it's crowded, accommodation can be expensive, and restaurants and attractions can be busy. By contrast, off-peak season is typically quiet, albeit a little lifeless, plus the weather can be bad and restaurants can be shut. Shoulder season (part way between peak and low), on the other hand, is often a perfect balance of decent weather but without the crowds – and is my preferred time to travel.

Avoiding peak season – especially over public holidays like Christmas, Thanksgiving, New Year, Easter and regional holidays in your destination (such as Golden Week in Japan and Chinese New Year across Southeast Asia) – can help bring the cost down too, or if you must travel then, it's advisable to book ahead to make sure you have somewhere (good) to stay. Likewise, low season can see the prices of flights and accommodation drop considerably and advance booking is not always required.

Always check for local festivals, celebrations and events when planning your travels too. I found myself heading to Montezuma, on the coast in Costa Rica over *Semana Santa* (Easter week – the busiest week of the year) – along with what felt like every Costa Rican in the country. The buses and ferries were packed, the area was practically fully booked in terms of accommodation and it was all I could do to find a hotel that wasn't extortionately-priced or already booked up. I learned the hard way that a little forward planning goes a long way during busy times, so do your research and book ahead when required.

In Vang Vieng, Laos, on Christmas Eve, I came across a weary traveller who had just arrived in town without pre-booked accommodation, to find no rooms available. It turned out the town was so busy – not because of Christmas, which the Laotians don't celebrate – but because of a Korean music festival taking place that weekend. So, it's always worth making sure you have somewhere to stay before setting off for a new destination.

What will it cost?

The cost of travel around the world varies hugely, and you can live like a king for months in one country for the price of a weekend break somewhere else. Some budget travellers take this to extremes and will avoid some great destinations based solely on cost. But don't let cost alone put you off a place, instead try to find ways to factor in short stays in expensive countries. For example, can you camp rather than staying in a hotel? Are there any free activities, tours or museums you can take advantage of? Can you cook your own meals rather than eating out?

If a country is expensive to travel in, make the most of a region by exploring cheaper neighbouring countries. An all-inclusive package or tour can be a good way to keep a cap on spending – especially if you can get a discounted last-minute price, or travel in low season (when demand – and therefore the prices – are lower). Alternatively, can you travel as a group to reduce the cost per head? Hire a car together, share the driving and split the cost four ways; hire a villa for a week instead of booking individual hotel rooms; charter a boat or a guided tour – you might be surprised at how affordable it can be.

Visas and vaccinations

Be sure to check if you need any visas, vaccinations or anti-malaria medication before you head off.

Visas

Do you need a visa to get into any of your selected countries? Requirements vary depending on what passport you hold, and can change, so check with the relevant embassy in plenty of time, giving yourself ample time to apply and send your passport off if necessary, bearing in mind you might need to send your passport off to more than one embassy.

Some applications can take a few weeks to be processed and if you need a visa for more than one country, you'll need to wait until your passport is returned from one embassy before you can apply to the next. You might also need to request *invitation letters* from the country you intend to visit so allow time to gather any documents and fill in the forms too.

When applying for a visa beware of visa companies who will try to scam you by charging a fee to process your application. For British citizens, the Foreign Office website contains detailed advice about visa requirements and the associated fees and is a great first port of call: www.gov.uk/foreign-travel-advice

Some countries have a visa-waiver agreement with other countries or offer a visa on arrival for a fee – this is much easier than having to send your passport to the embassy, but it is advisable to find out in advance if there is a fee (details will be on the country's embassy website) and take the relevant cash. Payment is often in US dollars, so it is always worth taking some US dollars with you in case you don't have any local currency on arrival. Never rely on paying by credit or debit card – at best you might be directed to a nearby ATM, or bureau de change, which will be unlikely to offer you the best rates.

Crossing borders is often a time-consuming and bureaucratic process, but I have had one or two entertaining experiences too! When I was crossing from Northern Thailand into Laos, a uniformed border guard approached my travel partner and me, asking us where we were from and where we were going. It all seemed very official – then he proceeded to pull out his phone and ask for a selfie with us!

At passport control in Mexico, the border agent smirked when he looked at my passport – unsure what was so funny (my photo is not THAT bad!) it turns out that Sarah Kerrigan is also the name of the protagonist in the computer game **Starcraft**. She even looks a bit like me too!

Another time, when crossing by sea from Chetumal, Mexico into San Pedro, Belize, all passengers were verbally assigned a number that we had to remember. On docking at San Pedro, we were told to get off the boat and line up in numerical order on the quay, before proceeding one by one to the immigration counter. It took a while so officials even encouraged us to buy a beer from the kiosk whilst we were waiting! I have no idea why it had to be in such a specific order, but it was a fun way to get to know our fellow passengers and it certainly makes for an amusing anecdote!

Vaccinations and anti-malaria tablets

Once you've looked up the visa requirements, check the NHS Fit For Travel website (www.fitfortravel.nhs.uk/ destinations) for vaccination recommendations for the countries you plan to visit and make an appointment with your travel nurse in your GP's surgery or local travel clinic. It is advised to make your appointment two months before you travel as some vaccinations require a course of injections. Leave it too late and there might not be time to develop the antibodies your body needs to build up during a course of injections, so it's important you schedule this in.

Be aware that when visiting countries where yellow fever is present, you must carry with you a yellow fever vaccination certificate or you may be denied entry to countries visited subsequently. Always keep your certificate with your passport and don't lose it as it's valid for life and is an official document.

Check online or ask your travel nurse to find out whether malaria is present in your intended destination as you'll need a prescription for anti-malaria tablets if so. Different drugs are available so ask your travel nurse which is the best one for the countries you'll be visiting.

Remember you may need to start taking any tablets before you arrive in a country where malaria is present and continue for a few days after you leave, so always read the instructions carefully and follow the pharmacist's advice.

Vaccinations and anti-malaria medication can also be expensive so find out the cost in advance and factor it into your budget. Shop around for the best price too – your GP may charge a different price to your local travel clinic and supermarket pharmacy counters are often cheaper than high street pharmacies for malaria tablets. Your travel nurse may be able to advise where best to buy. Whatever you do, don't try to cut costs by scrimping on your jabs and anti-malaria medication: it's not worth risking your health – or even your life – for the sake of a few hundred pounds!

How to schedule your time

When you first start researching your destinations, you might want to try to see it all. You'll feel like you have all the time in the world and start making plans for each day. However, take it from me that you *can't* see and do everything, and you'll tire yourself out if you try to do too much! You'll enjoy it far more if you selectively choose where to go and what to see – don't try to pack too much into your itinerary.

I'd also recommend allowing some flexibility in your itinerary for your plans to change. Perhaps you'll fall in love with somewhere or someone and decide to extend your stay. On the flip side, somewhere may not be as good as you'd hoped, and you might decide to move on early. This is only possible if your plans are not fixed and you've not pre-booked/pre-paid for everything – or it could get expensive if you start abandoning your plans and cancelling existing reservations. Think about booking the essentials – some of the flights, the first couple of nights' hotel on arrival in a new destination and any tours that must be booked in advance, then leave the rest until nearer the time to allow for spontaneity and for your plans to evolve along the way.

Be aware that when entering certain countries, you sometimes need to provide proof of onward travel – i.e. your flight or onward transportation out of the country. You'll be asked to provide evidence of this at check-in and without it, you won't be allowed to board your flight, or you might be asked to buy an onward/return ticket from the airline right there and then — which can cost a small fortune.

If you really want to travel on a one-way ticket and see where the wind takes you, there are a few legal ways round this:

- For USD $12 **Best Onward Ticket** (https://best onwardticket.com) will purchase a fully refundable airline ticket in your name and then automatically cancel it after 48 hours. Whilst the ticket is active, you'll have access to a genuine booking in your name and you don't have to worry about cancelling it or waiting for a refund.

- Alternatively, you could purchase a cheap onward flight from a budget airline and then not take it. Use **Google Flights** (www.Google.com/flights) or **Skyscanner** (www.skyscanner.net) to check routes and prices before booking.

- If you're booking with air miles, it's often possible to cancel with no penalty and your miles and any taxes paid will be immediately refunded into your account.

- Or lastly, think about booking a fully refundable, flexible one-way onward ticket that you can cancel once you've cleared immigration at your destination. Bear in mind it might take a while for your refund to come through and be sure to check the small print when booking to ensure there are no cancellation penalties.

Remember to always check your destination arrival requirements before you travel to avoid any issues at the airport!

Other than that, once you're on the road, your accommodation reception, locals and fellow travellers will be able to give you tips and recommendations too, so don't be afraid to leave home without having everything booked.

RESOURCES RECAP:

- **The Best Time To Visit**
  www.thebesttimetovisit.com
- **Foreign Office website (UK):**
  www.gov.uk/foreign-travel-advice
- **NHS Fit For Travel**
  www.fitfortravel.nhs.uk/destinations
- **Best Onward Ticket**
  https://bestonwardticket.com
- **Google Flights** www.Google.com/flights
- **Skyscanner** www.skyscanner.net

5

WHAT TO PACK AND WHAT TO LEAVE BEHIND

It can be quite a daunting process to pack to go away for three, six, or twelve months – but in reality, you don't need any more for twelve months on the road than you do for two weeks. In short, you should take no more than you can comfortably carry, and you should also try to save some space for souvenirs – or just for that feeling that your stuff expands when you're travelling!

What you need

My advice would be to start with a sixty-five-litre rucksack – or medium sized suitcase – and one smaller twenty-five-litre rucksack for your hand-luggage. Any bigger and you will seriously struggle to carry it all around! You may prefer to travel with a wheelie suitcase but consider the type of places you'll be visiting before ditching the rucksack. I visited Railay in Thailand, which is only accessible by long-tail boat, and was expected to lift my luggage off the boat and wade to the shore whilst carrying it – there's no way this would have been possible with anything other than a rucksack (and even then, it was a precarious walk over slippery rocks to the beach.)

All possessions in tow – Railay, Thailand.

It may seem like a tough decision to leave behind your beloved possessions when you're packing to go away, but less really is more. When you're packing for the first time, it's easy to fall into the trap of trying to pack absolutely everything you need for the entire duration of your trip. However, unless you're travelling deep into a remote rainforest, or wild-camping up a mountain, you can buy pretty much anything you need on the road.

I remember arriving into Bangkok for the first time – my first destination on my first round-the-world trip – and I had six months' worth of toiletries and two bottles of sunscreen stashed in my bag. I later remember being surprised to see UK high street stores such as **Tesco** and **Boots**, plus big American brands such as **7Eleven** and **Circle K**, in addition to local supermarkets and pharmacies stocking global brands.

Plus, you can often buy things cheaper abroad than at home, so don't worry if you forget something. Buying toiletries once you arrive also means you haven't got to worry about leakages in your luggage, or annoying restrictions on liquids in your aeroplane carry-on luggage.

Dental appointments, haircuts and beauty treatments are also cheaper abroad, and they can often be done for the fraction of the price of what you'd pay back home. I remember paying the equivalent of five pounds for a haircut in Bangkok and thinking, *this would cost me forty in my usual salon in London!*

So, on to your packing list. This will obviously vary per person depending on the destinations you're visiting and the kind of activities you'll be doing, but as a general rule, take the following:

- No more than **seven days' worth of clothes**. Multi-purpose, multi-functional items of clothing such as **lightweight zip-off trousers** that double up into a pair of shorts can save space in your bag. Do your washing once a week.

- In warmer climates, you'll also need a **light coat or fleece**, a **waterproof jacket, two sets of swimwear, sunglasses and a sun hat**.

- **Two pairs of shoes**: one lightweight pair suitable for both wet weather and hiking and a pair of flip flops or sandals. Be brutal! You're unlikely to need bulky walking boots unless you're planning on doing a serious amount of hiking, so try to ensure everything you pack is multi-purpose and justifies its precious space in your bag.

In terms of equipment:

- **A mosquito net** (https://amzn.to/2t4nr0v). Remember to buy a 'double' size net if you plan on sharing a double bed with your travel partner.

- **A silk sleeping bag liner** – great to keep the mosquitoes off in hot weather when you can't face sleeping under the covers, or when staying in questionable hostels! (https://amzn. to/2MvYZ0b)

- **Two micro-fibre towels** – one for the beach and one for the shower (https://amzn.to/2lbYTyf)

- **A head torch** – great for camping, power cuts or visiting caves! Try this one from Pathfinder: https://amzn.to/2HTx5HG

- **Laptop** – for booking, blogging and keeping in touch. Go for a slim, lightweight model for easy transportation.

- **Smartphone** – take an old handset; you'll be less of a target for theft and less distraught if you lose it compared to the latest model! Make sure your contacts and any photos are backed up before you go.

- **MP3 player** – go for one with a long battery life and a decent amount of storage. Don't rely on streaming music as you won't always have access to Wi-Fi. Back up your music collection in case you lose or break your device. Hardware can be easily replaced; your music collection, less so when you're on the road.

- **Camera** – I love the waterproof **GoPro HERO** camera (https://amzn.to/2lbr6Fr). It's compact and you can take it underwater on a snorkelling trip.

- **Earplugs and eye mask** – good for long journeys, lie-ins and jetlagged naps during the day (https://amzn.to/2tcoRW4)

- **Medication** – including malaria tablets as required.

- **Toiletries** – but keep it to the minimum and travel light!

- **Sunscreen** – just one bottle, you can always buy more on the road.

- **Insect repellent containing DEET**

- **Hand wash clothes detergent** – for when you can't get to a laundrette.

- **A lightweight scarf or sarong** to cover up when visiting temples, to keep off the sun when on the beach, or for an extra layer if the temperature drops. It can also be used as a makeshift curtain or quick-drying towel in an emergency!

- **Kindle Fire tablet** – all the functionality you need from a tablet and e-reader at a budget price (https://amzn.to/2JGfr01).

- **First aid kit** (https://amzn.to/2yqynuH). See below for more details.

First aid kit

Even with decent medical cover included in your travel insurance it is worth packing a basic first aid kit containing the following items:

- Antiseptic wipes
- Hand sanitiser gel
- Antihistamine tablets
- Painkillers: paracetamol and ibuprofen
- Plasters and dressings of various sizes
- Burn gel
- Zinc-oxide tape
- Bite and sting relief cream and hydrocortisone cream (for stubborn mosquito bites)
- Water purification tablets
- Antacid tablets
- Loperamide (diarrhoea relief) tablets
- Rehydration sachets
- Petroleum jelly – prevents blisters and good for chapped lips
- Sterile syringes
- Small pair of scissors

With any luck, you won't need to use the serious stuff like the syringes, but if you are travelling in poorer countries that may not have plentiful access to sterile needles it is prudent to take your own with you just in case you end up in hospital.

The water purification tablets are also a precaution when travelling in countries where you cannot drink the tap water. You will almost always have access to bottled water but if, like me, you find yourself in Gunung Mulu national park in Malaysian Borneo after the shop has closed for the evening and thirsty after a day's hiking, you'll be grateful for being able to purify the tap water in an emergency!

Everything else should come in handy though, so don't scrimp too much on bag space for your first aid kit. The most common ailments to befall you will likely be minor cuts, grazes and burns, insect bites and upset stomachs, so go prepared.

Also, be sure to pack supplies of any prescriptions, including anti-malaria tablets, and make sure your vaccinations are up to date before setting off. For anything else, you should be able to pick up drugs and medicines over the counter in pharmacies around the world. Pharmacists globally usually speak some English and are a good first point of call if you find yourself with symptoms that you're unsure how to treat.

Getting a good night's sleep

I won't travel anywhere without earplugs and my noise-cancelling headphones – it's the only way I can guarantee myself a good night's sleep in spite of the pumping music from the bar across the street/loud traffic noise/barking dogs/crowing roosters/howler monkeys/call to prayer/people talking loudly in the corridor outside my room (delete as applicable – all the above have kept me awake at some point on my travels!) The world's a noisy place so be sure to pack earplugs!

Ten years of travelling the world led British composer and producer, KK, to create **Sleep Sound,** a soundtrack designed to help you sleep in noisy environments. Featuring calming rainfall, waves and waterfalls interwoven into a wall of soporific white noise; engineered to block out background noise whilst simultaneously coaxing you to sleep. To find out more, purchase or stream Sleep Sound, visit http://bit.do/sleepsound.

Monkeys!

Lastly, there will be a few possessions that you pick up along the way that will be indispensable to you...

In Bako National Park in Malaysian Borneo, the local monkeys – a confident troop of long-tailed macaques – weren't afraid of getting up close to the tourists to try to steal their food. Once, they even began chasing me when I was walking a trail in the park – it was terrifying! When relating this story to a fellow traveller, he said to me, *"get a toy snake. You know, one of the colourful children's toys that moves from side to side in a slithering motion when you hold it by the tail?"* Seeing my perplexed face, he went on to explain that monkeys are terrified of snakes and can't tell the difference between a real one and a toy – or rather they don't want to risk getting close enough to find out. So now I always pack a toy snake in my rucksack if I'm planning on heading to places where there are monkeys. I've also heard of people putting toy snakes on car dashboards in urban areas with a mischievous monkey population, to stop monkeys trying to enter and steal possessions from their cars – well worth the bag space, I'd say!

What not to pack

Here are some things you don't need – and this list is by no means exhaustive – but I'll share a few popular items on the naughty list:

- **Uncomfortable shoes** – take only comfortable, multi-purpose shoes that you can wear on more than one occasion and with more than one outfit.

- **Walking boots** – unless you have an extensive amount of hiking planned.

- **Perfume or aftershave** – in tropical climates it's just too hot and gets lost underneath all the sunscreen and mosquito repellent anyway.

- **Formal clothes** – will you really wear them and do you really need them? If yes, take smart, multi-purpose items that can be dressed up or down or worn more than one way. If you're on the move a lot, avoid items that will need ironing or have special laundry instructions.

- Those **neck pillows** for long flights – they're bulky and is it really worth carrying one around for your entire trip for the sake of a couple of long-haul flights? Just catch up on sleep once you have arrived and checked into your accommodation!

- **Hairdryers and straighteners** – if you really can't live without them, call ahead to your hotel and check whether they can provide one.

Try to avoid taking anything too valuable, unless you're sure you really can't live without it. Remember that you can pick most things up on the road so unless you're one hundred percent sure you need it, leave it behind!

Gift and souvenirs

If you're going to buy gifts or souvenirs, consider shipping them home, or waiting until the last minute before buying so you don't have to carry them around with you. It's tempting to buy things when you see them, but I would strongly advise you wait until your final destination, right before you leave for the airport, or you'll be lugging them round the world with you.

I decided to buy my friends and family beautiful silk and cashmere scarves at the beginning of my trip in Thailand and foolishly carried them round for two months until I travelled home. I should have just waited until the day before flying home to buy the gifts, as it turned out they were available to buy in every market across the country and took up valuable bag space and weight allowance.

Poste Restante

On the subject of posting items home, you may find it useful to know how to receive post when you are away. **Poste restante** is a service offered by many countries worldwide, where the post office holds the mail until the recipient comes to collect it. It is a great solution if you have no fixed address, are visiting somewhere temporarily, or are unable to receive mail directly at your place of residence and need to arrange to have a package delivered.

The duration items will be kept and instructions on how to address your letter varies per country so check out this useful Wikipedia article for country specific details: https://en.wikipedia.org/wiki/Poste_restante.

Alternatively, if you've already got your accommodation sorted, it may be easier to have the package delivered to your hotel.

RESOURCES RECAP:

- **Mosquito net** https://amzn.to/2t4nr0v
- **Silk sleeping bag liner** https://amzn.to/2MvYZ0b
- **Microfibre towel** https://amzn.to/2lbYTyf
- **Pathfinder headtorch** https://amzn.to/2HTx5HG
- **GoPro HERO** https://amzn.to/2lbr6Fr
- **Earplugs and eye mask** https://amzn.to/2tcoRW4
- **Kindle Fire tablet** https://amzn.to/2JGfr01
- **First aid kit** https://amzn.to/2yqynuH
- **Sleep Sound** http://bit.do/sleepsound
- **Poste Restante** https://en.wikipedia.org/wiki/Poste_restante

6

TRAVEL HACKING

I love the planning process of booking a trip. Researching everywhere I've always wanted to go; creating a shortlist and making the choice; figuring out the best travel route and searching for flight deals; finding the best places to stay and things to do then weaving it into a plan and seeing my itinerary take shape.

It can be quite overwhelming in the beginning, understanding which airlines fly the route I want to take, whether there's a cheaper or better way to get there, deciding whether to buy a cash ticket or spend air miles... so to help you get the ball rolling, here are some of my top travel hacking tips – sourced from personal experience, frequent flyers and some advice picked up along the way.

Cheap flights hack

When you're looking for the best flight deal, there needs to be an element of compromise between price, convenience and airline – so you're unlikely to find that the cheapest flight is also the most conveniently timed and with your favourite airline.

Think about whether it is more important for you to:

- **Travel as cheaply as possible** (even if it means arriving at your destination in the early hours of the morning or building in lengthy layovers to the total journey time).

- **Depart or arrive at a certain time of day** (perhaps your hotel has a check-in deadline which prevents you arriving after a certain time, or maybe you're just not a morning person/night owl).

- **Fly with your favourite airline** (to accrue frequent flyer miles and tier points, for the service or safety record).

If your travel plans are set in stone, get the flights booked as soon as your itinerary has been confirmed. Flights are unlikely to get cheaper but will certainly go up in price as seats become scarcer. If you have some flexibility in your plans, it could pay to wait and see if an airline launches a flash sale – more on that later.

I was once travelling from Koh Lanta in Thailand to Langkawi, Malaysia and made the mistake of booking flights way in advance, before I realised there was a much quicker and more convenient minivan and ferry route. The flights took me via Phuket and Kuala Lumpur, which were really far out of my way! The traffic was terrible, I was sitting for hours on a coach and then had to take a three-hour ferry ride. If I'd taken the local connections the journey would not only have been quicker and much cheaper but covered far less ground!

If your plans are not fixed, see how things pan out before booking. If you're travelling in low season, last minute availability on buses, boats and planes is not a problem so you'll have the flexibility to book last minute. Peak season travel will usually require advance booking, however.

Here are a few tips to help you get the most for your money when you're ready to book:

Use Google Flights

Google Flights (www.Google.com/flights) is a great starting point when it comes to beginning your flight search. You will see at a glance which airlines serve any given route; whether there are direct flights (or if you need to consider a layover), the departure times and the price.

You can filter search results according to the number of stops, the airline, the departure or arrival time, the price and the total journey duration. You can also pull up a price chart for the whole month so if you have some flexibility you can match your travel dates to the cheapest fares.

Never book one-way long-haul flights if you can help it! If you want to fly into one city and out of another, multi-city tickets with layovers are always cheaper than one-way flights. Bear in mind too that a stop-over can be more than just a few hours between flights in an airport – it could be a few days or a few months, so think creatively when planning your itinerary.

Once you have found the flight deal for you, you can click through to the airline booking page directly from Google Flights to complete your transaction. When booking flights, always buy direct from the airline, rather than from an online travel agent or third-party booking site. Booking direct from the airline usually offers the cheapest prices and means making changes to your journey is much easier – whether purchasing seats, modifying or cancelling your reservation.

If you find a third-party aggregator that is cheaper than booking direct with the airline, jump on the phone to the airline telesales team who are usually able to price match. If not, one of the main causes for price differences between sites is that they are comparing different fare classes – the booking site might be quoting you for a fixed, inflexible hand-baggage-only fare – versus a semi-flexible fare including a checked bag. Booking direct with the airline will usually offer you the most up-to-date availability and most accurate prices, so if a third-party site is coming up with cheaper fares, it often means that fare is no longer available and you'll likely have to pay the difference later if you book it.

The importance of booking direct is greatest, however, when things go wrong caused by reasons out of your control. If you have booked direct with the airline, they have a responsibility to resolve the problem, but if you've booked via a third party, the airline will just ask you to contact them – even if your booking is for that particular airline!

Stay a Saturday night

Staying a Saturday night puts you into a different *fare bucket* and usually brings down the price of a trip, so if your Monday to Saturday trip is looking expensive, try adding an extra night and watch the price drop.

Presumably, the rule is there to profit from business travellers, who are travelling on business during the week – which is paid for by their employer. Saturday night, being mainly a *leisure* night, separates the business from the leisure travellers – so even if you're booking flights for pleasure, departing a day or two later could drop the price considerably. It's not guaranteed but is always worth checking.

The rule is perhaps a little archaic, but it can also work in your favour. When you're on an extended trip, the days of the week are less important and it's less urgent to be somewhere on a set day of the week, so you should be able to play around with dates to find the cheapest fares.

Holiday packages

In addition to staying a Saturday night, there are other ways to book into a lower fare bucket, thus saving yourself money on the price of the flight. One such way is to book a *holiday* package with the airline. Both British Airways and Virgin Atlantic offer good holiday deals.

Booking a holiday package means booking a hotel or car hire along with your flights. There are specific fare buckets that airlines offer solely to customers booking holiday packages so it's possible to get some cheap flight deals this way. You may even find adding just one night in the cheapest hotel available to your booking is enough to lower the cost of your flight significantly enough that you don't even need to stay in it – however, it probably makes more sense to stay there since we're not in the business of wasting money.

It's also worth noting that holiday packages remove the Saturday night requirement if your travel dates fall mid-week and are fixed. When booking a holiday package you only need to pay a deposit, with the balance being due a few weeks before your departure date.

Finding the best deal requires patience, determination and the willingness to play around with lots of different options to see if you can make it work – but the persistence can really pay off and save you money on your trip.

Book during airline sales

Whilst I generally prefer to book as soon as my plans have been finalised, airlines do launch scheduled and flash sales throughout the year – often with very competitive prices – so keep an eye out for these and see if you can bag a bargain. If airlines are on sale at similar times they will often try to compete with each other to win your custom so compare deals in the first instance using Google Flights.

Sign up to airline mailing lists to be kept informed of sale dates and destinations before they happen, and keep your ear to the ground around key sale periods, such as Black Friday and the January sales. Be prepared to act quickly as the fares won't hang around for long and seats on popular routes will sell out quickly.

On the lookout for the next British Airways sale? The **Continental Club** blog (http://blog.continentalclub. co.uk/) predicts sales based on historical data and looks at previous sale fares, so you know what to expect and if you're getting a good deal or not.

Fly for less with a partner airline

Booking a flight with a partner airline on a **codeshare** agreement can sometimes result in cheaper tickets than booking direct with the original airline – even for a seat on the exact same flight, aircraft and departure time.

There will be a dual flight number – one for each airline, but it should be noted on the booking page whose plane you will be flying on. You will still earn air miles and tier points when flying with a partner airline so it's always worth comparing airlines to see if you can get it cheaper. The reason for the price difference is usually a discrepancy between the fares, taxes or fees charged by the two airlines.

Before making a booking, check out which other airlines are in the alliance and search for codeshares. There are three main alliances:

- **Star Alliance** (www.staralliance.com) is the largest alliance with twenty-eight member airlines including Lufthansa, United Airlines, Air New Zealand and Singapore Airlines.

- **One World** (www.oneworld.com) has fifteen airlines including British Airways, American Airlines, Cathay Pacific and Qantas.

- **Skyteam** (www.skyteam.com) has twenty members including Air France, Delta and KLM.

Virgin Atlantic is not part of an alliance though they are partners with a number of airlines including **Delta, Air New Zealand, Air China, Singapore Airlines, Jet Airways** and **South African Airways,** meaning you can earn and redeem Virgin Flying Club miles on all the above airlines.

It's also useful to know the partners and alliances of any given airline in the event of cancellations or modifications to your flight itinerary, as you may be able to transfer onto a partner airline at no additional cost if your flight is cancelled.

Think of these tips as the tools in your arsenal. They may not guarantee you cheaper flights, but the more you understand about how the system works, the better your chances of playing it to bag yourself a bargain.

When comparing deals and itineraries, you can sometimes be confronted with a bewildering array of airlines and options, so, if you're not familiar with an airline or their safety record, the **Airline Ratings** website (www.airlineratings.com/airline-ratings) is a useful resource. It compiles a safety rating (out of a maximum score of seven stars) for each airline, based on an in-depth analysis of data from the world's aviation governing body (the **International Civil Aviation Organization**), key air travel associations (**International Air Transport Association** and the **Federal Aviation Authority**); along with government and crash data.

Airlines are sorted alphabetically – simply click into your chosen airline and read the score breakdown, which is based on a number of factors, including whether they are endorsed by governing bodies; if they appear on blacklists which prohibit them from flying into certain territories; whether there have been any fatalities in the last ten years; adherence to safety parameters and other considerations. It's technical but the star rating should give you a good indication of how safe it is to fly with any given airline if you're a nervous flyer.

Flying into Mexico City.

How to earn air miles without taking a flight

Air miles are not just for frequent flyers, they are an effective and flexible way of reducing the cost of travel and you don't even need to fly to build up an air miles balance! The great news is that you can also earn air miles whilst your feet are firmly on the ground. When I first took an interest in travel hacking, I didn't need to fly much, so here's what I did to start the ball rolling.

Before I begin, a quick caveat: if you're going to use solely this method to earn air miles you'll need to be patient, as it takes time – but you will be rewarded in the long run. So far, I've had lots of *free* flights (for both my travel companion and me) using only the methods below. (Oh, and when I say free, I mean the ticket is technically *free*, but I still had to pay the government fees, taxes and Air Passenger Duty – still, it's not bad considering the cash value of the ticket.)

If you're just starting out, I'd advise you to pick one airline and devote your air mile earning efforts to that one account. Don't spread your energies over multiple airlines if you want to start redeeming as soon as possible. Start by considering who your preferred airline is. If you don't have one, think about which carriers operate out of your local airport; look at the routes they fly and think about whether they are places you'd like to visit.

Virgin Atlantic (www.virginatlantic.com), for example flies to many USA and Caribbean destinations, but only a small number in Asia and none in Europe.

British Airways (www.britishairways.com) on the other hand, covers most destinations worldwide and has an excellent coverage of the UK and Europe – so if you're more interested in redeeming your air miles for European city breaks, you'd probably be more interested in a British Airways Executive Club account. Avios, the currency used by British Airways Executive Club is also used by other airlines including Aer Lingus, Vueling and Flybe, and points can be transferred between accounts for more earning and redemption opportunities.

Lastly, consider if your favourite airline is part of an alliance – that means you're allowed to earn and spend miles on code share, or partner airline flights, as I discussed in the previous section. It's great to be able to shop around and pick the most suitable flights for your schedule or budget and know you can still be able to earn or redeem air miles.

Once you've made your choice, go online and set yourself up a frequent flyer account with your chosen airline and make a note of the number – you'll need this to hand for the earning methods below.

Credit cards

Credit cards are a great way to boost your air miles, and perks for card holders can include sign-up bonuses, companion vouchers, free upgrades, travel insurance and airport lounge access in addition to miles for virtually every £1 spent. Sometimes the sign-up bonus alone is enough to redeem for a free flight immediately! To put this into perspective, when it comes to spending your miles, a return trip from London to Europe with British Airways starts from 9,000 miles; and London to the USA with Virgin Atlantic costs from 20,000 miles for the round trip, with you paying only the associated taxes and fees.

One of the most valuable benefits is arguably a two-for-one companion voucher, where you can take a friend for free on a redemption flight. If you do most of your travel solo, however, this perk may be worthless to you so shop around to find perks that best suit your travel lifestyle. To find out more about the credit card options available to you, check out **Head For Points** in-depth travel credit cards directory: www.headforpoints.com/best-uk-avios-airline-hotel-credit-cards

Affiliate shopping

You may be familiar with cashback websites, through which you can earn cash back on every purchase, but did you know you can also earn bonus air miles on your everyday shopping via airline affiliate shopping portals? British Airways' portal is called **Gate 365** (www.shopping.ba.com) and Virgin Atlantic's is **Shops Away** (www.virginatlantic.com/gb/en/flying-club/partners/shopping/shops-away.html). Simply click through to your preferred retailer via your airline's shopping page then earn miles for every pound you spend.

The number of miles earned per pound varies per store and can fluctuate with promotional offers, but many high street and online names are included, such as department stores, travel websites and car rental companies. You can also earn miles on insurance products, flowers, photo printing...and the list goes on!

I regularly click through to **Booking.com** (www. booking.com) or **Hotels.com** (https://uk.hotels.com) when I'm travelling so I'll earn a handful of air miles for every hotel booking I make. It's a free and easy way to earn air miles (provided you're going to make the purchase anyway – it goes without saying you should never purchase something you don't need just because you can earn a chunk of air miles.)

The miles can take a few months to post to your account, but provided you don't need them in a hurry, it's a good way to keep your account topped up for very little effort. So, whenever you shop online, get into the habit of checking if you can earn affiliate miles and you'll soon see your mileage balance skyrocket.

If you shop at **Tesco** in the UK and Ireland, you can also convert your **Clubcard** points to British Airways Avios or Virgin Flying Club miles. Collect 600 Avios or 625 Virgin Flying Club miles for every £2.50 in Tesco Clubcard vouchers. For more details visit: https://bit. ly/2rxzXF3

Be aware that air miles do have an expiry date (thirty-six months in the case of British Airways and Virgin Atlantic but it can vary for other airlines). However, earning just one air mile is enough to keep your account active, thus extending the life of all the miles in your account, so shopping online is a great way to prevent your miles from expiring when you haven't got any flights planned.

Surveys

If you've got time on your hands, for example on a long commute, or even whilst you're watching television, you may enjoy doing surveys at **E-Rewards** (www.e-rewards.com) or **Rewards for Thoughts** (www.rewardsforthoughts.co.uk); where you can earn points for completing surveys – that can be converted into air miles.

With **E-Rewards**, you typically earn a few hundred points per completed survey and a nominal number of points if you don't qualify for the survey. Once you have a certain number of points you can exchange them for Avios or Virgin Atlantic Flying Club miles.

Rewards For Thoughts, on the other hand, offers twenty-five or fifty British Airways Avios points per completed survey. The Avios points post directly into your British Airways Executive Club account within a few days of completing the survey.

To sign up, visit the URLs above or log into your British Airways or Virgin Atlantic account and follow the links to find out more.

Hotel stays

It is also possible to convert loyalty points from major hotel chains into airline miles. Hilton, Marriott, IHG,

Starwood, Hyatt, Shangri-La and Radisson all offer this option. You can even choose to credit some stays directly to your frequent flyer account. Log into your hotel points account and check the small print, or ask next time you check in. However, be sure to weigh up whether you're likely to get more value from the points as complimentary hotel nights or air miles – you'll need somewhere to stay after you take that free flight anyway!

If you're a few thousand miles short of a hotel redemption, remember you can purchase points to top up your account – look out for flash sales and bonuses. Redeeming points on hotel nights can offer excellent value, especially during peak travel seasons, where cash prices for hotel rooms can soar – whereas the points value of a room remains fixed throughout the year.

There are also third-party hotel booking sites such as **Rocketmiles** (www.rocketmiles.com), **Kaligo** (www.kaligo.com), **PointsHound** (https://pointshound.com) and **Agoda** (www.agoda.com/avios) that reward you with air miles for each booking. There's a sign-up bonus for booking your first stay and points are rewarded per pound spent thereafter. Shop around to make sure you're getting the best deal amongst all the sites and bear in mind that you will forego any hotel loyalty/status points or perks by booking via a third-party site.

Car rental

Similar to the hotel set-up, it's possible to earn air miles through car rentals, and both British Airways and Virgin Atlantic partner with major car rental chains so you can earn frequent flyer points on your car hire reservations.

The official partner of British Airways Executive Club is **Avis** (www.avisba.com) and Virgin Atlantic partners with a number of car hire chains including **Alamo**, **Hertz**, **Avis**, **Enterprise** and **Sixt**. Check out www.virginatlantic. com/gb/en/flying-club/partners/car-rental.html for more details.

Before making a booking, always scout around for the best deal – which may be a better value cash deal that does not accrue airline points. Also look out for seasonal deals or promotions offering discounts or air miles bonuses – but factor in more than just the mileage earning potential to find the deal that's right for you.

With a little dedication and a combination of the above methods, you can start building an air miles balance to go towards your first redemption. Turn it into a habit and your air miles balance will grow on a monthly basis, even when you're not flying.

Purchasing miles

You can buy Virgin Atlantic Flying Club miles and Avios via your online frequent flyer account, however, I would only recommend it if there's a particular redemption or upgrade that you're saving up for; if you're a few thousand miles short when you want to make a booking. If you're in no rush to redeem your miles on a flight booking, it is best to let your account balance build up organically. Purchasing miles is ultimately a way of making your airline ticket more expensive and should be reviewed objectively.

Whatever your timeframe on your travels, start earning the air miles now and you might just earn yourself a free flight sooner than you think.

Miles rack up even faster when you start earning via flying too. Note that purchasing one long-haul British Airways return flight will probably earn you enough miles for a free short-haul redemption when you get home! The more you fly, the more you earn – and the more you earn, the more you fly! It's a great feeling when you can pay for the majority of your flights with your miles – and hugely cut down on the initial outlay when booking your next trip.

How to fly business for the price of economy

Travel-hacking enthusiasts use a variety of techniques to get more for their money which can mean they can fly business class for the price of economy, and I want to share with you some of their methods. Before I begin, please note that a little flexibility and a lot of determination are required, but if you can make it work for you, you might just be able to give up flying economy for good and really transform your air travel experience! Here are some other tips to help you maximise your money.

Fly out of a European hub instead of London

London may be well-connected, but when you're planning a long-haul trip, consider starting your journey in Europe instead of the UK – and especially from London. This is because Air Passenger Duty (APD), taxes and fuel surcharges vary per city and London is one of the most expensive cities in the world.

Often it is much cheaper to start your journey from a European capital, even though you could be directed back through London to connect to the long-haul leg of your journey. Using Google Flights, play around with departures from alternative cities and you may be surprised how much you can bring the price down.

Factor in the ease of getting to the European city to see if it justifies the inconvenience of starting your journey there and check the total price to see if it justifies the saving – especially if you need to book a flight, hotel and airport transfers into town to get there – all of which eat into your budget. When looking at the total cost bear in mind that you'll be charged in your departure country's local currency, so consider the exchange rate and whether you'll be charged any foreign transaction fees on your credit card.

If it makes economic sense, why not add an additional stop to your itinerary and start your trip with a European city break in your departure city? Just make sure you factor in some contingency in case of delays as if you miss the first leg of your trip, the remaining sectors will be cancelled.

I was once looking for return flights from London to New Zealand over Christmas and found some for over £1,000 cheaper by flying out of Prague. Of course, you'd need to get to Prague in the first place and then factor in the associated costs such as airport transfers and hotel, but £1,000 was a huge saving that could justify the added leg to the journey.

Time is the main requirement to accommodate flying out of alternative cities as it's vital you don't miss the first leg of the itinerary. For example, if you have a flight booked to Singapore from Dublin via London, it's not an option to just pick up the flight from London. Missing the Dublin to London leg would result in the whole itinerary being cancelled. You must factor in enough contingency to get to Dublin, which may require an overnight stay, depending on the time of your flight the next day, or at the very least, a few hours' layover to allow for delays. Alternatively you could plan an extended stay of a few weeks or months in your stopover destination before you move on.

This applies to some extent in economy class too, but you'll often find cheap promotional business class fares from EU-based airlines who are prepared to offer cheaper fares than your home airline to win the business.

I've used London as an example as it's where I'm based but you can apply the same principles if you live elsewhere. Wherever you are in the world, consider if there's a nearby city or airport you can fly from for a cheaper deal.

Insider and expert tips

FlyerTalk (www.flyertalk.com) is an online forum for everything associated with travel, and especially anything to do with air miles and travel tips. You will also find beginners' guides to earning and spending air miles and points, so swot up on the basics and dive into the conversation.

It can take a bit of getting used to – the navigation is not obvious and there are hundreds of threads across lots of different forums but take some time to find your way around and you'll find it an invaluable resource for news, tips and insider information.

Every now and again *incorrect* (read: super cheap!) or *error* fares are loaded onto airline booking systems and are available for booking. These are spotted by eagle-eyed flyers and shared with the forum, albeit somewhat cryptically – but take some time to learn the lingo, understand the jargon and you'll soon be fluent in frequent flyer language!

Airlines will usually honour these error fares, but you have to be quick as once the airline has spotted the mistake, it will soon be corrected. As an example, a friend of mine was able to travel from Barcelona to Costa Rica return for £500 in business class – basically the airline missed off a zero when loading the fare... it goes without saying that the fare did not stick around for long, but the airline did agree to honour it.

If you stumble across an error fare, don't be afraid to book right away as British Airways has a twenty-four-hour grace period, in which you can cancel a booking with no penalty. If you can't decide between two sets of dates – book both and then just cancel the one you don't want within twenty-four hours! This rule applies to flight bookings but it's worth double checking the terms and conditions before buying holiday packages as they can have varying conditions depending on whether it has been booked online or over the phone.

Head For Points (www.headforpoints.com) is my favourite travel journalism site for everything points related (from a UK perspective). Sign up to the mailing list and you'll receive daily emails with the latest news stories, deals, offers, reviews and competitions.

There are regular reviews of the latest credit card offers, hotel sales and bonus points promotions, the best available deals in airline sales as they happen, and other ingenious ways to earn and spend air miles. You will also find introductory guides to points and travel hacking (for those new to the game); reviews of hotels, airlines, airport lounges and a whole host of other travel related products and services. What editor Rob doesn't know about collecting points and travel hacking in the UK probably isn't worth knowing!

Whilst much of the theory behind travel hacking is not country specific, many of the practical tips and applications for putting it into practice depend largely on your location, so it's worth researching a blog that covers your region. For readers based in the USA, **The Points Guy** (https://thepointsguy.com), **Travel Codex** (https://travelcodex.com) and **Frugal Travel Guy** (www.frugaltravelguy.com) are all great resources for maximising travel and points. Even if you can't find a travel blog or travel hacking tips for your specific region, you can still benefit from generic tips and advice or airline deals available in a location you plan to visit.

Earn status and get upgraded

Did you know that if you fly regularly and have **status** with an airline, you are statistically more likely to be offered an upgrade than someone who is not a member of the frequent flyer programme?

Better still, if you have status and are close to moving up a tier, the airline is probably even more likely to consider upgrading you if there is space – to give you a glimpse of the benefits of the next level and to encourage you to put in the effort to go up to the next tier.

Upgrades are selected by the airline's computer system and contrary to popular opinion, it doesn't matter what you're wearing or whether you ask for an upgrade for a special occasion – it's ultimately the computer that decides.

To maximise your chances of an upgrade, check in as soon as your flight opens. It doesn't matter if you have pre-selected seats in your original (economy) cabin – you are still in the running for an upgrade, but the first to check in, will usually be the first in line for an upgrade. If you're travelling with someone, you'll be upgraded together – airlines don't tend to split up a travel party – though statistically, upgrades are more likely to happen to single travellers as one free seat in a premium cabin is more probable than two together.

The main thing that affects your eligibility for an upgrade, however, is how full each cabin is. If the economy cabin is oversold but there is space in premium economy or business, the airline will look at which passengers to upgrade from economy to premium or business. If it's full in premium economy and business, but empty in economy there is therefore very little chance of an upgrade. There are forums on Flyer Talk that can check the flight load (i.e. the number of tickets sold in each booking class), so delve deeper if you want to tactically increase your chances of an upgrade on strategically *empty* flights.

If you are keen to upgrade, ask at the check-in desk on the day of travel to see if there are any paid upgrades available. These will often be at a fraction of the cost of the upgrade if purchased in advance and are only available on the day of travel. An airline will always offer upgrades to those willing to pay for them (albeit a nominal fee) before they give them away for free. Of course, you're under no obligation to purchase so there's no harm in enquiring when you check in!

Checking in as soon as the flight opens also massively increases the chance that you will fly if the flight is oversold, as the last passengers to check in are usually the first to be offloaded. If you are in the unfortunate scenario of the flight being over-booked and are asked to take the next flight, never settle for the first offer of compensation! It is common for airlines to incentivise passengers to persuade them to take an alternative flight.

If you are offloaded, can you negotiate airport lounge access whilst you wait for the next flight? How about seeing if they can upgrade you to business class and fly tomorrow if you can't have your economy seat today? Don't settle for the first cash offer – on more than one occasion I have witnessed airlines increasing the cash compensation incrementally until they have enough passengers willing to be offloaded. It's part of the beauty of having open-ended travel plans – you can enjoy the extra perks and fly on a quieter flight just for being flexible! I have been in this position on a couple of occasions – and was usually interested in taking the compensation and being flexible in my travel plans – however, the uncertainty and change of plans is not for everyone and my travel partners have twice talked me out of it – another argument for travelling solo!

But let's just rewind a little and I'll spend a moment explaining status. Airline status rewards frequent flyers by awarding them **tier points** for every qualifying flight they take. The airline, fare class and the distance flown determine the number of tier points earned. Tier points are collected in addition to air miles and the more tier points you collect in your membership year, the higher the level of status you will achieve. A level of status expires after one year, though it is possible to earn lifetime status in some cases – but if you're just starting out, let's not get ahead of ourselves!

Some of the benefits of having airline status include priority check-in, fast-track security, additional baggage allowance, airport lounge access, priority boarding and an enhanced air mile earning rate, (depending on the airline, or alliance you're flying with). Status is transferrable within an alliance and varies between airlines, so check with your frequent flyer scheme what the benefits are and where you can take advantage of them.

Some travellers *chase* status by constructing complex travel itineraries that consist of a series of connecting flights, which together earn a large number of tier points, flown solely with the intention of earning enough tier points to retain a certain level or status, or to achieve the next level of status. This is known as a **mileage run**.

The complexity of the mileage run depends on the level of status required – it could be a few well-planned flights, or a complex, multiple-leg itinerary in which flyers don't see much more than the inside of an airport or an aeroplane. In any case, it's useful to know that a certain tier of status can be guaranteed with a few strategic flights and if you've got a lot of travel planned, the perks of airline status can make flying a much more comfortable experience – whether through reduced queueing, free champagne in the airline lounge or priority boarding.

Use airline miles to part pay for your ticket or upgrade

If you have a pile of airline miles, then don't just sit on them. **Earn and burn** is the best strategy!

Unless you have a particular redemption that you're saving up for, consider using your miles to upgrade your ticket to a higher class of travel, or do an outright redemption for the full ticket and just pay the taxes. Redemptions are subject to availability so consider booking up to a year ahead (reservations open exactly 355 days in advance for British Airways and 330 days for Virgin Atlantic) to guarantee availability, particularly if you are booking multiple seats in the premium cabins.

Many airlines also allow you to redeem a handful of air miles to reduce the price of the ticket by a few pounds. If you take this option, you will still earn miles on the flight, so when part paying with air miles it is possible to earn back as many – or more – miles when you take the flight, especially when combined with the increased earning rate in the premium cabins.

Keep an eye out for **reward seat sales** which offer discounted redemption rates to really maximise your miles.

Also consider travelling **off-peak** to reduce the number of air miles required for a redemption. Peak and off-peak calendar dates vary between airlines – even within the same alliance – so it's worth shopping around airlines in that alliance if your dates are fixed; or playing around with dates to get the greatest value from your miles.

Miles4Migrants

Lastly, if you find yourself with a load of air miles that you don't need or can't use, consider donating them to **Miles4Migrants**, a not-for-profit charity that uses donated air miles to fly refugees to their new homes.

The minimum donation is 10,000 miles but most refugees will need up to 25,000 miles to fly to their new home, in addition to taxes and fees. If you have more miles to donate, Miles4Migrants tries to fly families together on the same ticket in a single redemption.

You can also make cash donations to cover the taxes and fees associated with airline tickets or use the forum to connect people you think might be able to assist with the programme. Miles4Migrants will notify you when the refugees have successfully flown using your miles and have been reunited with their family in their new home. To donate or find out more, please visit www. miles4migrants.org.

Now your flights are sorted, let's look at life on the road and I will share my top tips to get to grips with your new nomadic lifestyle.

RESOURCES RECAP:

- Google Flights www.Google.com/flights
- **The Continental Club blog** http://blog.continentalclub.co.uk
- **Star Alliance** www.staralliance.com
- **One World** www.oneworld.com
- **Skyteam** www.skyteam.com
- **Airline Ratings** www.airlineratings.com/airline-ratings
- **Virgin Atlantic** www.virginatlantic.com
- **British Airways** www.britishairways.com
- **Head For Points credit card directory** www.headforpoints.com/best-uk-avios-airline-hotel-credit-cards
- **Gate 365** www.shopping.ba.com
- **Shops Away** www.virginatlantic.com/gb/en/flying-club/partners/shopping/shops-away.html
- **Convert Tesco Clubcard points to airline miles** https://bit.ly/2rxzXF3
- **E Rewards** www.e-rewards.com
- **Rewards For Thoughts** www.rewardsforthoughts.co.uk
- **Rocketmiles** www.rocketmiles.com
- **Kaligo** www.kaligo.com
- **PointsHound** https://pointshound.com
- **Agoda** www.agoda.com

- **Avis** www.avisba.com
- **Virgin Atlantic car rental partners** www.virginatlantic.com/gb/en/flying-club/partners/car-rental.html
- **FlyerTalk** www.flyertalk.com
- **Head For Points** www.headforpoints.com
- **The Points Guy** https://thepointsguy.com
- **Travel Codex** https://travelcodex.com
- **Frugal Travel Guy** www.frugaltravelguy.com
- **Miles4Migrants** www.miles4migrants.org

7

LIFE ON THE ROAD

You've done all the planning, booked your flights and you're finally off on your adventure! Here's what to expect when you hit the road.

The pace of long-term travel is wildly different to a holiday, so give yourself time to settle in and consider what it takes to give you the energy to keep going. This could be days with nothing planned – spent lying on a beach with a good book, healthy eating days, days abstaining from alcohol, working days, admin days, the opportunity to sleep in or get an early night... whatever it takes to reenergise and sustain you.

Wherever you are in the world, there will be times when you need a few home comforts. Look after yourself so you don't end up with travel fatigue – stay healthy and well-rested and allow yourself time to stop and take stock.

Enjoy the difference and variety that your trip throws at you and immerse yourself in local culture. Living like and learning from the locals is all part of the travel experience so embrace it and enjoy the fact that it's a far cry from your life at home.

Here are some tips to make your life on the road a smooth journey.

Money

Staying on budget

The life you lead when you're travelling – the glamour, or the lack thereof – is largely dependent on the budget you've set and the countries you're travelling in.

Whatever the duration of your trip, it's important you stick loosely to your budget. Allow some flexibility for once-in-a-lifetime experiences and activities – subsisting alone can be relatively cheap, wherever you are in the world, you can cook your own meals and enjoy low cost or free activities such as sitting on the beach all day with a good book – but when you start adding on the tours, entry tickets and restaurants it can really begin to drive up the cost.

In some countries, you'll be able to live like a king (five pounds for a full body massage in Thailand, anyone?) But equally there will be countries where you'll be penny pinching to simply stay on budget (for example in Australia, the cost of basic accommodation like camping is comparable to a four-star hotel in Cambodia).

For me, the memories of zip-lining over the cloud forest in Costa Rica or jumping 224 metres from the Macau Tower in the world's highest bungee jump are easily worth the expense, but just don't sign up to every tour going (especially when your accommodation starts giving you the hard sell.)

World's highest bungee jump – Macau, China.

Your budget should give you the flexibility to do a few extras and factor in the unexpected higher living expenses of some countries on your itinerary, but it's important you have a fixed amount each month that links back to your original budget (which you refer to regularly) to make sure you stay on track, or you might find yourself needing to head home sooner than expected.

When I was travelling in New Zealand, I got chatting to a backpacker who was overjoyed to have just found work – albeit cleaning in a meat processing factory in the small hours of the morning! So desperate was he for work, he would accept anything just so he could continue his travels! This illustrates why it's so important to budget carefully and to allow yourself a buffer in case things don't work out quite as planned. Don't be that guy – I think he was vegetarian too...

Cash is king

Cash is your best bet when spending abroad, especially outside of the main cities where credit cards are not always accepted. There's usually a local currency ATM at the airport, but in case you can't find one, or the machine is out of order, always carry a few US dollars/ euros/Great British pounds with you. If possible, take some local currency with you – just enough to pay for a taxi from the airport, one night's accommodation and a meal on arrival.

If you are going to rely on credit card use (especially if you want to boost your air miles balance), do it before you depart on your travels. Pay for your flights, book the hotels you need to cover the first few nights when you arrive, buy any travel gear and vaccinations you need. After that, credit cards are best kept for emergencies and on the off-chance that you can use them – certainly don't rely on them and always endeavour to carry some cash with you, even if it's just a few US dollars.

Haggling

If you're used to living in a country where everything has a fixed price, then getting used to handling money, haggling, and paying for your shopping can be one of the biggest culture shocks when you're on the road.

It's important to at least have a go at haggling when purchasing items as socially, it's the way business is done in certain parts of the world. The haggling process is like a dance, enabling both the buyer and seller to reach a satisfactory outcome.

When you find something you want to buy, find out the going rate for the goods by asking around at a few shops/stalls and comparing the goods on offer. Start by asking the vendor how much, knowing that he will begin with an inflated price, then make a counter-offer, which he will then counter – and so it goes on until you meet somewhere in the middle.

Only make an offer on something if you are serious about buying it and consider how much you're actually prepared to pay for it. As a rule of thumb, I commonly counter with an offer of one third to one half of what the vendor quotes me, knowing full well that he has over-quoted me in the first place. I usually end up paying somewhere around two-thirds to three-quarters of the price he offered me initially. Some vendors drive a hard bargain, others fix their prices with other traders, so everyone pays the same, but it's important to at least go through the motions even if you end up paying the asking price.

Selling strategies

Look out for the following strategies employed by market traders and see if you can use them to your advantage to strike a good deal.

- In some parts of the world, the first sale of the day (especially if it takes place before midday) is considered a lucky omen. Superstitious traders may drive a hard bargain to get their "lucky" first sale. See if you can negotiate a good deal for yourself by giving it to them!

- Sellers claiming to be about to shut up shop for the day, will try to convince you to buy there and then, or you'll miss out on today's "special offer".

- In an attempt to entice you in, some shop owners will offer you free samples or show you hospitality, but don't feel pressured into buying – you don't owe anyone anything.

- Watch out for opening tactics, where vendors build rapport by making jokes, engaging you in conversation, claiming to be your friend or a relation of someone you know. Once there's a relationship, it can seem difficult for you to refuse to make a purchase without appearing rude but remain firm and don't be afraid to walk away.

- Some vendors will appear to be hurt by your opening offer but play them at their own game by looking shocked if you are quoted a price you consider to be way too high. A little theatre can go a long way and it is all part of the routine.

- When you've agreed to buy something, check that the seller doesn't switch the item you have selected for an inferior one. It's easy to take your eye off your purchase when you're fumbling for your purse in your bag and the seller is bagging your item. If in doubt, keep hold of it whilst you hand over the money and let the seller offer you a bag to put it in.

Haggling tips

- Ask for a discount if you are buying in bulk. Most sellers are prepared to offer a discount if you're buying multiple items.

- Play "*good cop, bad cop*" with your travel companion: you express an interest in an item and your shopping partner tries to talk you out of it (in front of the vendor). It might persuade them to make you an offer to get you to buy right away.

- Always be prepared to walk away – if you have made a reasonable offer, the vendor will usually come after you to negotiate.

- If you are being bothered by people giving you the hard sell, don't be bullied into buying. Sellers know their persistence can convince you to buy just to make them go away! Equally, if you just want to browse, make it clear you are *just looking*.

- Feign disinterest in an item – the more interested you appear, the higher the price!

- Don't try to screw sellers over – it may seem like small change to you, but those few extra cents will make more of a difference to him than to you. It may feel like all traders are out to scam you, but most are just trying to make an honest living.

- Smile – be charming and polite. Rudeness or aggression won't get you anywhere.

- Have fun and enjoy the process!

Food market – Chaing Rai, Thailand.

Tipping

It's also worth taking a moment to research tipping etiquette before you arrive in a country. Just as refusing to haggle – and consequently overpaying for goods – is bad for the local economy, over-tipping is not encouraged for the same reason (as it leads to an inflated price for other tourists and for locals too). In some countries, such as China, tipping is neither desired nor expected as it can be embarrassing for the vendor and implies that his employer does not pay him well. In some cases, tipping is even illegal. By contrast, failing to tip your taxi driver in New York City will result in a very unhappy (and underpaid) driver – who relies on tips to top up his salary.

Remember you are supporting the local economy, so whilst you may be travelling in cheap countries to make your budget stretch as far as possible, don't be so cheap that the local community doesn't benefit from your tourism. Workers in some sectors are paid a very low wage and in some countries, there is no such thing as a minimum wage. Be sensitive to local economies and be aware that what a Thai minivan driver may earn in a day may be equal to the price of your morning coffee back home. When I was travelling in Thailand I had some scary minivan journeys – being driven up to fifty kilometres over the speed limit, taking sharp bends way too fast and on the wrong side of the road, often with no seatbelts fitted in the vans... Consider then, the difference (to your life and his) if you offer him a small cash incentive – say, equal to his daily salary – if he is prepared to stick to the speed limits and get you there safely? Discretion is key: it's never a good idea to shout abuse at the driver and embarrass him in front of the other passengers – that will likely make him continue to drive just as fast. Instead, ask him at the next stop, out of earshot of other passengers. He'll be grateful for the extra cash and you might feel like you've been spared another hair-raising journey.

A home from home – finding the best place to stay

There's often a bewildering choice of accommodation to choose from when you visit a new location. I usually start my accommodation search by opening up **Booking.com** (www.booking.com), **Airbnb** (www.airbnb.com) and **TripAdvisor** (www.tripadvisor.com) and inputting my travel dates. This gives an initial indication of the price range and what I'll get for my money. I then apply filters on price and location, sort by customer rating and then spend most of my time reading customer reviews. There is a lot of average accommodation out there, from hostels to five-star hotels, so I look for the wow factor – it could be the friendly management, the rooftop pool, the central location or the best facilities.

What are your top priorities when looking for a room once you take budget out of the equation? Do you want to be in the thick of it, in the centre of town where the bars and restaurants are, or in a sociable hostel where you can meet lots of other travellers? Do you want to be sure of a peaceful night's sleep? Perhaps you want to be close to nature or public transport links? Or something else entirely!

Of course, you'll need to read between the lines in customer reviews as everyone has a different idea on what makes the best (or worst) place to stay. There's always someone who wants five-star luxury for rock-bottom prices, or someone who gives a bad review just because the Wi-Fi is a bit slow...

For me, I like to guarantee a quiet night's sleep and be within walking distance of the centre of town, or where the shops, bars and restaurants are – but far enough away to ensure the loud music from a bar isn't going to keep me awake until four in the morning. Cleanliness is a top priority. A private bathroom and air conditioning are a bonus – but by no means deal-breakers. What are your accommodation must-haves?

Some of my favourite accommodation has been bare bones, but in the most amazing locations: staying right on the beach in a bungalow in Koh Lanta, Thailand, falling asleep to the sound of the waves, with nothing but a bed, a fan and a mosquito net for £8 per night– it's basic but the best spot on the island.

When to book

I think it's usually worth booking in advance – it saves you from having to lug around your bags from hotel to hotel when you arrive to see if they have vacancies and if they're within your budget. Booking ahead gives you peace of mind that you'll have somewhere to stay and a decent indication that you have somewhere nice if you've done your research. On the other hand, many travellers prefer to find somewhere when they arrive, and they often end up with cheaper (last-minute) prices. Not every hotel or hostel advertises online, of course, so there are often some real gems available to discover when you get to a new location. Perhaps a half-way house (if you'll pardon the pun) is to book your first night to guarantee you have somewhere to stay when you arrive, then once you've dropped off your bags you can go out in search of somewhere to stay for the next few nights.

When choosing a hotel, always ask to see a room before handing over the money. Check the room for noise (is it next to a loud bar or can you hear noise from the room next door?) and also for security (do the locks work and is there a safe?)

In some countries you won't get past immigration if you don't have proof of accommodation, so if it's your first night in a new country, you'd be advised to check the entry requirements, or just book somewhere to be on the safe side. When I was in Rarotonga in the Cook Islands, I needed to provide proof of booked lodgings in order to clear immigration at the airport. I heard horror stories from other travellers about how people had been turned away at the border for not having booked accommodation in advance– and put back on the next flight out of the country. Imagine travelling all that way to somewhere so remote only to be turned away for something as simple as not having booked a room! It wasn't a case of there being no available accommodation, but a way for immigration to account for tourists' whereabouts – so make sure you're aware of what's expected of you on arrival in a new country.

Bed bugs

In tropical parts of the world, it is advisable to check for bed bugs before checking into a room. They may be more notorious in budget accommodation but are not discerning, and an unfortunate infestation could mean they are just as likely to plague a five-star hotel as a hostel dormitory. To check for bed bugs, pull back the sheet and check the corner of the mattress for small blood stains. Lift and drop the corner of the mattress and you might see the little critters (the size and shape of a flax seed) scurry away.

Tell-tale signs of an infestation are bites – not dissimilar to mosquito bites, but in a straight line. If you're unfortunate enough to find yourself in a room with bed bugs, you'll need to make sure you don't take them with you to your next destination – or you could permanently infest your bag and clothes for the duration of your trip. If you're worried your clothes might have come into contact with bed bugs, wash them on a hot wash. If you don't have access to a washing machine or have delicate garments that are hand-wash only, put them in a black bin bag and leave them out in the sun (if you're in a country with a tropical climate). The heat will kill off the bugs without damaging your clothes.

Taxi card

When you've found a place to stay, pick up a business card from reception, or do a *pin-drop* of your location on your map app on your phone. This can come in handy if you get lost and can't find your way home or need to give directions to a taxi driver that doesn't speak your language. Ask your hotel reception to write down the name and address of the lodgings in local language and provide a phone number. Hotels in China give out what's known as a *taxi card* with the address written in Chinese characters, to save any confusion when getting a taxi home, without needing to ask for directions.

We can't stay here!

Sometimes, no matter how much research you've done, or how many reviews you've read, you'll end up staying somewhere that's not as described – albeit filthy, or just downright weird.

My first time in Hong Kong I inadvertently checked into a guest house in the infamous *Chungking Mansions* – little did I know that its reputation preceded it and a film, **Chungking Express** (https://amzn.to/2teALP4) has been made about it!

Chungking Mansions holds Hong Kong's record for the most guest houses in one building, packing in nearly two thousand guest rooms in total. Its cheap prices and central location make it a popular choice for backpackers and budget travellers, but the communal areas leave a lot to be desired.

My room itself was clean, quiet and featured everything I could need in a central Hong Kong residence; however, to get to it, I had to wind my way through a dingy shopping centre and take a tiny, cramped lift to one of the top floors of the building.

The lift was always packed to capacity and contained people from all walks of life: from weary tourists dragging heavy suitcases, to enterprising locals carrying giant tubs of curry. The landings and stairwells were squalid, filthy areas, often frequented by unsavoury or suspicious looking characters. I think I even stepped over someone smoking a crack pipe in the stairwell... Fortunately my stay was only for a few days, so I stuck it out but I was pleased to finally check out.

If you find yourself staying in a dodgy guesthouse, don't feel particularly safe or are unable to lock the door, a top tip is to carry a wooden or rubber wedge in your bag – if the door to your room opens inwards, wedge it shut from the inside to stop anyone on the outside getting in. It's simple, effective and doesn't take up much bag space.

The kindness of strangers

One of the great joys of travelling is meeting and interacting with locals and people from different cultures and walks of life. Where possible, always try to step outside of traveller circles and spend some time interacting with locals. Staying in locally run guesthouses or bed and breakfasts can provide a great opportunity to get to know your hosts – and for them to get to know you.

When you're used to living anonymously in a big city, it's easy to mistake offers of kindness and generosity for someone trying to take advantage of you. Whilst it's wise to beware of scammers it's important to remember that most people are generally good. Wouldn't you hand in a wallet if you found it on the street, run after someone if they dropped something to return it, or give directions to a lost tourist in your home town?

I once left my debit card in an ATM in Tulum, Mexico – a silly mistake, yes, but, I inadvertently walked away from the machine when I had taken my cash, forgetting in Mexico that the card is the last item to be returned from the ATM. I withdrew the cash in the morning and didn't realise I didn't have my card until the end of the day. Fortunately, on returning to the bank, some kind soul had spotted my card sticking out of the machine and handed it in at the counter. I would have done the same, of course, but it's easy to assume the worst of people when you are in a sticky situation in an unfamiliar environment.

In the Yasawa Islands, Fiji, my travel companion and I went to hire a snorkel and mask and the shopkeeper offered to take us out in his boat to snorkel around an atoll just offshore. Initially my defences were up, and I declined, thinking about how we shouldn't go off with strangers, but I soon realised he was just trying to be nice and give us a better snorkelling experience. In any case, everyone on the island knew him and our accommodation had recommended we hire the snorkels from him. We spent a fantastic hour, him acting as our guide, pointing out manta rays, colourful fish and corals – so much richer an experience than we would have had on our own.

In Vang Vieng, Laos, our accommodation host cooked all her European guests' dinner and threw us a party on Christmas Eve, so we could celebrate and wouldn't feel homesick. We drank shots of her mother's home-made *snake brandy* (home brewed liquor with a snake or giant centipede inside the bottle for decoration – or, according to our host, flavour!) and enjoyed hearing her anecdotes of life growing up in Laos, as we shared our stories with her.

Disclaimer: Of course, it's important to follow your instincts and if something doesn't feel right, then don't do it! Be open to the experience but don't put yourself at risk if your gut feeling is telling you to be cautious. If in doubt, seek advice from locals, take a friend along with you and let someone know where you're going or what you're doing.

For an authentic cultural experience, take the time to get to know the people you meet. Assume the good in people. Always respect local customs and traditions. Be grateful, humble and don't take advantage of their generosity. Your travels will be all the richer for it.

Getting around

Wherever you are in the world, you'll probably have a few travel options available to you. As with anywhere, a taxi is going to be more expensive than a public bus and a flight will cost more than a long-distance coach, so in addition to price, you'll need to factor in convenience and how much time you have.

One of the benefits of long-term travel is being able to embrace *slow travel*. Stop rushing, take the scenic route, travel with locals and take in the views – see more than the inside of an airport or aeroplane when travelling somewhere! It's amazing what you notice when you're not rushing from one place to the next and allow life to happen to you along the way.

When travelling from Chiang Khong in Northern Thailand, over the border to Luang Prabang, Laos I had to choose between the forty-eight-hour slow boat and the overnight sleeper bus – each option had its benefits and its challenges. I took the bus and the views over the mountains were stunning, however I found myself being driven round some very steep, precarious and pot-holed mountain roads – I even saw a lorry that had flipped over onto its side after taking a bend too fast – and consequently wished I had taken the boat! However, on speaking to someone on the boat, they said two full days and nights in an upright seat takes its toll – even on the beautiful Mekong River!

In some countries, you'd be advised to take the train or a tuk-tuk, hire a car or scooter, rent a bicycle or simply walk everywhere. I always try to embrace the local culture and travel like the locals – it's the cheapest way to get around and sometimes it's a real experience too! I'll never forget trying to sleep on a Vietnamese overnight bus, despite the loud karaoke music blaring out all night. The elderly lady in the seat next to me sang her heart out throughout the journey! On a long-distance train journey across Vietnam I nodded off and woke up to find two locals sitting on the end of my bunk, making the most of somewhere to sit to eat their breakfast after I had inadvertently curled up into the foetal position as I slept!

Weigh up all the options to see what works best for you and don't be afraid to make the journey part of the adventure. Use blogs and online forums in advance of your trip to help determine the best way to get around. A quick Google search should get you off to a good start and once you're on the road, ask your fellow travellers for their tips and experiences.

Taxi scams

When it comes to being scammed abroad, travellers' tales of taxi scams are often at the top of the list. All the guide books tell you to only use authorised, or official cars, to check driver registration documents, always use a meter or agree a price upfront – but somehow it still goes wrong for us sometimes. Experienced scammers attempt to use these tactics on people all the time so when you're in a new or unfamiliar place it's all too easy to get caught out.

I took a taxi from San Jose, Costa Rica to nearby town, Alajuela. After I ensured I got in a licenced cab, the driver made a point of turning on the meter and making sure I could see it. What later caught me out was him insisting on me paying by credit card then charging me in a different currency to what he quoted me in. With hindsight this seems rather obvious that I should be charged in the local currency! It all got very confusing – he told me I was paying in US dollars, but he charged me in Costa Rican *colons* – and with my luggage still in the boot I didn't want to risk making too much of a fuss and him driving off with my bags in tow. So, I ended up paying approximately double for the trip and chalking it up to experience – the silver lining being that having paid by credit card I was able to flag the transaction with my credit card provider and get my money back.

The moral of the story is to be aware and never to put your own personal safety at risk. Try not to let one bad (taxi) experience ruin your trip and don't assume that all taxi drivers are out to get you – most of them are out to earn an honest living and are kind, considerate people. If you are scammed, put it down to experience, spread the word to your fellow travellers so it doesn't happen to them and move on. More serious incidents, however, should be reported to the local police.

To minimise the chance of being scammed, find out the approximate cost of the journey in advance and agree it up front with the driver. Pay with cash and tender the exact fare if you can, so there's less opportunity for a driver to short-change you (or pull the classic "I don't have any change" excuse!) If you are getting a taxi to your accommodation, have the front desk book one for you as they may work regularly with a reliable driver who is known to the hotel – and who wouldn't want to risk damaging his relationship with the hotel by ripping off its guests.

A cautionary tale about toilets...

One of the biggest changes to adjust to when you leave home for a life on the road is bathroom habits and etiquette. Firstly, you had better get used to throwing toilet tissue in a bin – or you'll be calling your hotel maintenance and explaining how you've blocked the toilet. In many developing countries the antiquated pipes are just not built to process anything other than human waste.

Secondly, depending on where you are travelling (but especially in Asia), sooner or later you will come across squat toilets – essentially holes in the ground. Men clearly have the advantage here. For female travellers it's an art form to perfect – and one that I struggled to manage when wearing trousers. It doesn't take much imagination to conceive what went wrong for me when trying to use a squat toilet on a moving ferry in choppy waters!

When I chatted to a female traveller who had just returned from a trip to Hampi, India, she regaled me with the horrors of queuing in a long line of ladies at a long-distance coach stop, all waiting to 'use' a hole in the ground in the centre of the room. There were no cubicles, the floor was wet with urine and with several more hours' travel time on the bus ahead of her, there was no choice but to await her turn to do her business in front of everyone. Not fun at the time, but she survived to tell the tale and can now see the funny side!

So, ladies, let me recommend to you SheWee, (https:// amzn.to/2yfXqjR) a simple travel device that literally enables you to urinate whilst standing up and without removing any clothing. However, a caveat: please don't hold me responsible for any odd looks you get from confused locals and travellers alike when using the ladies' toilets – I am not sure what the local Indian ladies in Hampi might have made of this, had it been available!

Communication

Arriving in a new and unfamiliar country is a bit like reverting back to childhood: you struggle to make sense of what is going on or how things work and are unable to communicate effectively. It always pays to learn a few phrases and key words and a smile goes a long way if there is a language barrier. It helps endear you to the locals if you are seen to be making an effort with basic greetings, please and thank you, but it can also be a life-saver when you need a few basic directions or advice when English is not commonly spoken.

It is easy to fall into the trap of assuming that everyone can at least speak a few words of English – let me assure you that this is definitely not the case! You will become an expert in gesticulating by the end of your trip! A pocket phrase book, flashcards with pictures of everyday items, or access to a language app on your phone is recommended, although beware of needing an internet connection to look up words or expressions as you will probably find it is not available when you need it most!

If you decide to learn a language before you go, I really like the Michel Thomas method (www.michelthomas. com) – he breaks it down in a practical and logical way, so you can figure out how to construct whole sentences based on their component parts. It's an audio course with no textbooks and no note-taking, which makes it ideal to learn over headphones whilst you're on the move.

You may prefer to do an intensive course at a language school whilst you're in that country. Courses tend to be flexible and you can attend for as long or short a duration as suits you, but you'll probably need at least a few days to begin to get a feel for having basic conversations with confidence. A Google search or enquiry at the tourist information office will help you find local language schools in your area.

In some corners of the world, you will encounter fascination from the locals – whether it's your *funny* hair, skin tone, height, or style of clothes – you will feel a bit like a tourist attraction yourself from time to time. I've had people come up to me asking to take my photo, wanting to practise their English, or asking me about the Queen and her corgis (who I simply must know, if I'm from London!) Children will shout, "*Hello, how are you?*" or other phrases they have learnt at school as you walk past in the street and love the opportunity to engage (though they will often go all shy when you smile and answer them back). Perhaps one of the oddest responses I had was from the children in Cambodia, whose response, on me telling them that I was from England, would be "*I'm from Scotland!*" I'm still not sure what this was from, but it was a popular English phrase in Cambodia!

On visiting Vietnam, my father-in-law found himself being treated like a bit of a celebrity, with locals coming up to him, asking for photos and old ladies reaching out and touching his stomach. Amused and interested about why he might provoke this kind of reaction in people (and his wife having had no such interest from the people) it was later explained to him that his *big belly* reminded them of the Buddha and they believed touching it would bring them luck!

RESOURCES RECAP:

- **Booking.com** www.booking.com
- **Airbnb** www.airbnb.com
- **TripAdvisor** www.tripadvisor.com
- **Chungking Express** https://amzn.to/2teALP4
- **Shewee Extreme** https://amzn.to/2yfXqjR
- **Michel Thomas method** www.michelthomas.com

8

STAYING HAPPY AND HEALTHY

Health

A few precautions and a little common sense can go a long way to keep you healthy on your travels. Some basic practical advice can keep minor afflictions at bay and if the worst happens you'll be covered by travel insurance. Read on for tips on staying happy and healthy on the road.

Travel insurance

Travel insurance covers everything from medical expenses to trip cancellation, lost luggage, accidents and other losses incurred while travelling. As soon as you start booking flights and accommodation, make sure you also buy travel insurance – then you're covered in case of airline and hotel insolvency or cancellation before your trip begins. To get the best deal, use a comparison website, or if you already have travel cover, speak to your current provider to see if they can also provide cover for longer trips.

Not every insurance company provides *backpacker cover* so check before you buy. And even if you're not technically planning on backpacking, check what type of cover is available for longer stays. If you plan on travelling, living, or working abroad longer-term, consider getting *expat health insurance.*

Factor in the type of activities you plan on doing whilst you're away. *Dangerous sports* are not always covered so do check in advance if you plan on doing activities like scuba diving, canyoning, bungee jumping or sky diving. You can usually add on an activity for a nominal fee but it must be declared in advance.

You must declare any existing medical conditions at the time of purchasing your travel insurance and keep it updated it with any diagnoses, treatments or changes in medical history as they happen. Failure to do so may invalidate your policy, which could result in you being denied treatment or being hit with hefty medical bills, if you try to claim and the insurance company refuses to pay out.

Once you have the itinerary for your trip, it's also worth checking with your home contents insurance provider too as many policies have a restriction on for how long you're permitted to leave your house empty. Obviously, this won't be a problem if you have someone checking in on the place, or tenants living there, but do bear in mind that longer periods of absence can invalidate your policy in the event of making a claim.

When insuring your possessions away from home, make sure the cover you select is adequate and note the excess payable should you need to make a claim, along with per-item limits. It is possible to get specialist photography and computer insurance if you plan on taking expensive camera equipment, or a laptop that you can't afford to lose, whether for work or play.

The best advice, however, is to not take anything with you that you can't afford to lose: especially sentimental, irreplaceable or unique items. For everything else, make sure you are adequately covered.

Sickness

During your travels, it is almost certain that you will experience an upset stomach at one time or another. It's not just food or water that can cause the upset, sometimes it can be a simple reaction to the change in climate, diet and routine. If sickness strikes, try to take it easy for a few days. Eat plain, bland food, drink plenty of water, get lots of rest and stay away from anything that might aggravate your stomach including spicy or greasy food and alcohol.

One of the most common causes of sickness and travellers' diarrhoea on the road is through drinking the water, which includes ice in drinks and fruit or salad that has been washed in tap water. Always drink bottled or purified water and avoid ice or salads unless you can be sure that purified water has been used. Check the seals on bottled water before you buy, or it could mean the empty bottles might have been taken out of the bin and filled up with tap water in a bid by an enterprising and unscrupulous trader keen to earn a bit of extra cash on the side.

Before you arrive, it's worth checking online forums, with locals or your accommodation hosts whether it's safe to drink the water. Generally, you'll be fine across most of Europe, North America and Australasia but there are also some areas – for example, Medellin in Colombia, where you can drink the water, but you can't elsewhere in the country.

If you are heading to places with limited potable water, get a refillable water bottle with filter that you can refill from any fresh water source, like this one from GRAYL: https://amzn.to/2teI8Gn. With one press of a button, it removes 99.9999 % of all bacteria and viruses, and filters out any sediment, chemicals and heavy metals. The filter is exchangeable and last for three months. Think about refilling bottles and reducing plastic waste where possible, especially on islands where there's nowhere for the waste to go.

In countries where you cannot drink the water, ice is often bought in – you might see an ice truck doing the rounds in the town, making deliveries to bars and restaurants. Often though, there is no way of knowing if the ice is made from purified water, but if everyone is drinking it, you might decide to take the risk and you may well be fine – especially in an area popular with tourists. In Luang Prabang, Laos, in the central market there was a line of street vendors, all selling blended ice and fresh fruit smoothies – all made with ice and water and popular with locals and tourists alike. Technically there was no way of knowing if the ice and water was okay, but the popularity spoke for itself.

Fruit should be okay if it can be peeled and food should be cooked so it is hot throughout. Opt for popular restaurants or street food stalls with a high turnover of food and healthy and hygienic looking staff. Even better if you can see your food being prepared fresh before your eyes. In restaurants, check out reviews on TripAdvisor, or get recommendations from fellow travellers or your accommodation.

Don't forget to pack a bottle of hand sanitiser gel – in many countries it is customary to eat with your hands and alcohol hand gel can help prevent you from getting sick. If you have food allergies, look up the translations before you go so you can communicate clearly, even if you don't speak the language.

Eating and drinking on your travels is a great joy – keep it that way with these simple precautions.

Eating well

The food is one of my favourite things about travelling: trying local specialities is one of the best ways to get to know a new country. When you arrive at your hostel or hotel, ask the staff where the best local restaurants are. They will be able to direct you towards authentic cheap eats or fine dining.

As a general rule, I tend to avoid Western-style restaurants and chains. Not only is the food often not as good as the local fare, but it's usually more expensive and you are not supporting local businesses. Your guide book and fellow travellers will usually be able to give you some great tips on where to eat, so search out where the locals go and join them! It's often the best food and the cheapest too, so be adventurous and try local specialities at least once!

In Costa Rica, I ate cheap and plentiful home-cooked food every day in **sodas** – family-run establishments somewhere between a café and a canteen, often open twenty-four hours. For breakfast, I ate **gallo pinto**: rice and beans with fried eggs, plantains, toast and served with a large dollop of chilli sauce – all for a fraction of the price of a **full-English** or American-style pancakes in a Western-style café.

In Thailand, I ate steaming plates of pad Thai served fresh from night market stalls and in Vietnam, I slurped fragrant bowls of *'pho'* – or noodle soup – from big bowls at a pavement stall. From fresh croissants in France to dim sum in Hong Kong, eating the local specialities is rarely a disappointment, especially if the region has a reputation for good food.

"Casado" – the Costa Rican staple.

Arriving late at night into Singapore, I sought out a local café for a snack before bed. "Have the carrot cake!" the proprietors said. I was happy to go with their recommendation but bewildered when my food arrived, and it looked nothing like the carrot cake that I know and love so much back home! This *Singaporean* carrot cake was more comparable to the solid starchy substance you find in the bottom of the saucepan after cooking rice or pasta! I certainly won't be ordering that again, but I still laugh at the memory.

Perhaps my most amusing food incident was the *pad Thai* I had on Isla Bastimentos, Bocas Del Toro, Panama. The alarm bells should have begun ringing when the café owner said it was a Mexican dish and that it was usually his wife that did the cooking – but he would have a go at making it for us. Well, what we were served didn't resemble a traditional pad Thai in the slightest – I was presented with a sloppy, brown plate of tagliatelle smothered in peanut butter with a few pieces of chicken on top. The moral of the story is perhaps to eat local dishes instead of delicacies from the opposite side of the world!

So, order it, give it a go! The worst-case scenario? You might not eat much of it and order something different next time! However, you might stumble across a delicious delicacy – so be adventurous as you may never get a chance to try these foods again! Of course, there will be times where you really crave comfort food – for me it's jacket potatoes, or pizza – and you'll almost always have access to global cuisines, wherever you are in the world, but the rest of the time, step out of your comfort zone and try something new.

It might be a bit more of a *local* experience when travelling in a remote village, or on long-distance trains or buses, though that said, you can usually find a packet of biscuits and a can of fizzy drink if you're desperate! From broken down buses and transport delays, unrecognisable or unpalatable looking food for sale, to a simple lack of choice, I learnt the hard way that it's best to take food provisions with you on a long journey. Fellow backpackers have also regaled me with their stories of *overdosing* on Oreos in the absence of sustenance on long journeys, so it pays to go prepared. If you stop, or have the opportunity pick up something tasty along the way it's a bonus – just make sure you take something, or you could find yourself hungry and thirsty on a long journey.

Aside from the cost of eating, a longer trip isn't like a holiday, so you need to eat sensibly when you're travelling too. If you do what you do on holiday and enjoy three-course feasts in fancy restaurants every night, your waistline and wallet won't thank you for it! Eating nutritious food will help keep you healthy and support your digestive and immune systems, keeping you in good health on the road. Processed, fried or other unhealthy foods are often the easiest and cheapest option, so you need to try to make sure you're getting a balanced diet, even when it feels like a false economy.

Consider booking a self-catered apartment or hostel with shared kitchen, and cook your own meals. Not only is it often cheaper than eating out every day, but healthier too, as you can control what ingredients go into the meal. That's not to say you can't indulge too – so long as you're aware and try to maintain a balance.

I do miss the cooking experience when I'm travelling, so it's great to go self-catered and enjoy being back in the kitchen again. Cooking in a communal kitchen can also be a great way to meet people and share travel tips – great if you're travelling alone and don't enjoy eating on your own.

Bon appetit!

Exercise

It can be quite a lifestyle change to up sticks and go travelling – a real break to the routine. So, in addition to eating healthily, it's important to stay fit on the road – especially if you're used to regular exercise when you're at home – otherwise you may find yourself eating and drinking as if on holiday and could start piling on the pounds!

I don't tend to do formal exercise when I'm away, but often walk miles taking in the sights and wandering around the local area. However, I always throw in my running kit, so I can go out for an early morning run on the beach (before it gets too hot), do a HIIT (High Intensity Interval Training) workout in my hotel room, or find a locally-run yoga session.

I've found myself wanting to exercise more whilst on the road, but in a hot country it can just feel too hot and humid, so consider finding a class in an air-conditioned studio, or try swimming in the sea, or hotel pool.

Maintaining happy relationships with your travel partner(s)

They say that travelling with a partner will make or break the relationship – so pick your travel companion wisely, and perhaps go on holiday as a dry run before you hit the road for a year to check you're compatible.

By compatible, I mean do you have the same trip goals, ideals (around the standard of living on the road) and understanding of compromises to be made when it comes to travel on a budget? Do you both have the same budget in mind and what are your deal-breakers? You may be up for staying in dorms, or camping to travel as cheaply as possible, but your travel partner's benchmark accommodation may be a four-star hotel with air conditioning and a private bathroom, so give it some thought before you commit to go together. But most importantly, can you spend twenty-four hours a day, seven days a week with one person (or the same group of people) without driving each other crazy?

Positive and open-minded types make the best travel companions – someone who is good in a crisis; flexible and optimistic when things don't quite go to plan. It's important you work as a team when things go wrong – perhaps some accommodation is not what you hoped, and you need to check out early, maybe an enterprising local is trying to rip you off. Stick together through the good times and the bad and you'll come out of your trip in a stronger relationship.

It's probably a new experience to suddenly spend twenty-four hours a day in the same company, so it's wise to factor in some time apart – whether it's sitting in the same room but quietly reading or heading off in different directions for a while and doing your own thing. Learn what the other needs and how to get on best. Be kind and look after each other to get the most from your trip.

In fact, it can be wise to take some time out from other people and the tourist trail in general. Just as you don't have to be doing activities all the time, you don't have to be around people all the time either. Taking some time out will give you the opportunity to slow down, take stock, catch up on reading and enjoy your own company – it can be a great way to prevent burn-out, or travel fatigue. I'm an introvert and I need periods of solitude to reenergise and recuperate, especially on the busy tourist circuit.

Conversely, there will be times where you will rely on your fellow travellers for company, tips and advice, regardless of whether you're travelling solo, as a couple, with friends or in a family group. Hostels often have a communal area, or bar where you can meet other travellers and it's a great way to meet other people and pick up recommendations for your onward journey. Organised tours are also a good way to meet other people and are often the best way to see an attraction, when you need some time out, a change of scenery or company.

However, and with whomever you travel, enjoy the experience and the rich variety of characters you will meet along the way. It will make for a lifetime of great friendships and stories and you'll be talking about your adventures for years to come. So, cherish those memories and try not to get bogged down with other people's minor irritations. Revel in your differences – cultural or otherwise – keep learning and putting yourself in other people's shoes. Understand their customs and ways of living and you'll be all the more open-minded for it. Ultimately, as travellers and humans, we all have the same broad needs and wants, so be tolerant, be humble, be polite and be kind! Do unto your fellow travellers as you would have done to you.

Safety and security

In terms of personal safety, the same rules apply as anywhere in the world, i.e. don't put yourself at unnecessary risk by going out alone in remote areas late at night, or by flashing valuable possessions. You cannot avoid risk altogether and there's no way to be 100% safe, but you can mitigate it as far as possible.

Government travel advice

Before you set off, check government restrictions on travel, which can change regularly and at short notice. On my first round-the-world trip, I had a six-month gap between booking the flights and travelling to Bangkok. In between the planning and the departure, there was some unrest in the city. As the advice was to not travel unless necessary, I was able to keep my flight into Bangkok but then I changed my travel plans to cut short my stay in Bangkok and take the train over the border to Siem Reap, Cambodia. Often it can be a case of avoiding certain areas in a country or city centre, as opposed to the entire country, but it is wise to heed government warnings and advice, and understand the potential risks before you go.

The following website from the UK government contains advice on travel to cities and countries around the world, including the latest updates on terrorism, crime and security, strikes and demonstrations, health warnings and travel advice: https://www.gov.uk/foreign-travel-advice. Advice for US-based travellers can be found here: https://travel.state.gov/content/passports/en/country.html

Media bias

When researching your destination, look beyond the news and traditional media and get more than one opinion of the situation. Start with your guide book for generic advice about the areas you'll be visiting, then check out local news and other sources to get an up-to-date picture.

If you're concerned about your safety, check with your hotel reception, or get advice from the local tourist information centre, local residents, or other travellers before you go. Get a second opinion too – most people are friendly and are happy to help, but it's worth asking around in case their advice is incorrect or worse, they are trying to scam you.

Keep your ear out for local news too – I arrived in Bocas del Toro, Panama to hear of the murder of a tourist that took place on a remote beach on one of the province's islands. Tourists were still allowed to visit that beach but were strongly advised to exercise caution and report anything suspicious to the police. There was a strict curfew to leave the beach in the evening and since the incident the police had started patrolling the beach and the jungle trail that leads to it, so it was probably safer than it had ever been – but it was prudent to be aware of any potential risks or hazards and to take extra care, just in case!

Don't let scary news stories put you off too much, though – there will always be horror stories (even in the local newspapers at home!) If you believed everything you heard, you'd be too scared to step outside the front door each morning. Don't simply rule out an entire country – instead, do your research and try to plan your itinerary to avoid *dodgy* areas and mitigate risk. Travel during the day instead of late at night, take taxis instead of local buses, hire a guide or book onto a tour instead of sightseeing alone and leave your valuables in the hotel safe or locked in your room.

Theft and sickness are likely to be the two most common mishaps to befall you on your travels, but the risk of unfortunate incidents can be significantly reduced with some careful planning and some basic common sense. You will notice that most of the following advice can be applied in your home country as well as abroad. Generally speaking, travel abroad is no less safe than travel within your own country. What's important is that you don't put yourself at unnecessary risk and you keep your wits about you. Of course, you might just be very unlucky – and that's what your travel insurance is there for.

Top safety tips

- **Take an old smartphone** – they are invaluable for calls, maps, email, internet access and a half-decent camera but will make you less of a target for petty theft than those with the newest model.

When you're out and about, don't keep phones or wallets in your back pocket where pickpockets will have easy access to them.

- Consider buying a cheap, **fake wedding or engagement ring**, so if you are unfortunate enough to be mugged or happen to lose jewellery on the beach or in the sea, you won't lose anything of sentimental value that cannot be replaced. Wear costume jewellery instead of real diamonds and precious metals – or better still, don't wear any jewellery at all that might attract the eye of a thief! A fake wedding ring is also a useful purchase for unmarried couples sharing a room in conservative countries.

- If you're feeling vulnerable in your accommodation, leave a pair of **men's boxer shorts** lying on the floor of your hotel room – in the event of a break-in attackers think twice if they think there might be a beefy boyfriend staying in your room!

- **Research popular scams** that operate in the region you're travelling in and learn how to avoid them. Your guide book, Google, accommodation front desk staff and your fellow travellers are a great place to start!

- **Keep emergency information to hand,** such as your travel insurance details, contact details of a friend or family member back home and the phone numbers of the emergency services, your local embassy and your accommodation. Keep them in your wallet and backed up on cloud storage so you will always have access to them. Email your itinerary and insurance details to someone back home, so they can check in with you from time to time and alert the authorities in the event of an incident.

- **Lock up your valuables.** Before agreeing to stay somewhere, check your accommodation has locks on the doors, or if you're staying in a dorm, that you have a locker to keep your valuables in. Use slash-proof bags which lock and tether them to furniture, luggage racks or something immovable so no one can make off with them easily. Pack a combination padlock and a carabiner in your luggage – you never know when they might come in handy.

- **Stash some emergency cash.** Hiding some emergency cash in your travel kit and on your person can get you out of a sticky situation if you lose your wallet or are pickpocketed. Try rolling up a fifty-dollar bill and hiding it in the handle of a disposable razor or an empty toiletry bottle. If you've got a wad of notes, divide them up and keep them in a few separate locations throughout your possessions. You could also give a friend or family member back home a credit card or some emergency funds that they can transfer to you in a crisis.

- **Dress appropriately**, respect dress codes and traditions and try not to stand out by looking or acting like a tourist. In religious or conservative countries, keep shoulders and knees covered, avoid brash or offensive slogans on clothing, and both men and women should avoid going topless.

- **Don't talk to strangers!** Beware of telling people

you've only just met that you're new in town, or the name of the guest house you're staying in. Instead, make out that you've been in the area a while and give the name of a different hotel if asked. Sure, people might just be being friendly and making conversation, but a little white lie doesn't hurt, and it could protect you from an unscrupulous scammer or thief.

- **Don't get too drunk or high.** Enjoying a couple of drinks with dinner is one thing, getting smashed and compromising your personal safety is another. An unplanned trip to hospital after a big night out could also turn out to be very expensive! Local police and embassies alike take a very poor view on foreigners getting caught with illegal drugs or breaking the law, so steer clear of anything that might get you arrested.

- **Safety in numbers.** Buddy up and travel with others to feel safer; whether it's going on a tour, travelling long distance or out for dinner in the evening, it's good to know someone's got your back or an extra pair of eyes on your luggage when you feel like you're in a dodgy area.

- **Avoid conflict where possible.** If you're unlucky enough to find yourself being mugged or threatened with violence, just hand over your money or possessions and report it to the police. Don't try to fight back – it's just not worth the risk.

Health and safety regulations

You will find that many countries around the world do not conform to the rigorous health and safety standards of developed countries like the UK, USA and Australia. Hotel rooms may not be fitted with smoke detectors, carbon monoxide alarms are seldom seen and there are few regulations around portable appliance testing (PAT), a process by which electrical appliances are routinely checked for electrical safety.

It is not uncommon to see plug sockets in bathrooms, unearthed plug cables, or overloaded plug sockets in the communal area of a hostel – where everyone is trying to charge up their phone and laptop – and other precarious electrical situations that might not be considered safe back home.

As per usual in such situations, take care and don't expose yourself to unnecessary danger – better a drained phone battery than a trip to Accident and Emergency following an electric shock!

I recommend carrying with you a portable power bank (such as this one: https://amzn.to/2t9Ncvq) for charging your devices on the go. You can even buy portable carbon monoxide detectors – it might just save your life! Or course not every country and/or guesthouse will require it, but better to be safe than sorry.

Suicide showers

Costa Rica (and Panama) are famous for their "*suicide showers*", so called because the (unearthed) water heater is built into the shower head, rather than drawing the water from a heated water tank. Unearthed, with exposed wires and often held together by electrical tape; you are advised not to touch the shower head with wet hands – for obvious reasons!

Although commonplace in this part of the world, it's best to make your shower short and sweet. Don't fiddle around with the temperature gauge or touch the shower head – and if possible, avoid using it altogether!

Cold water showers are generally the norm in hot countries anyway, often with only higher-end accommodation offering hot water showers. A cold shower can be refreshing when you've spent all day in high-humidity and tropical temperatures, but I swear I'll never get used to a cold – or at the very best, tepid – shower first thing in the morning. Still – rather that than danger of death!

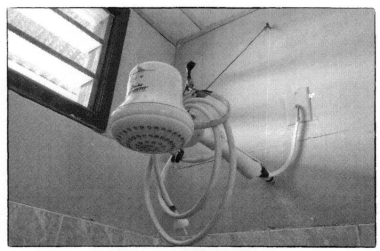

"Suicide shower" – Panama.

Coming home

The Life-changing element of travel

Long-term travel – or the act of taking off several months from your usual routine alone – offers you the time and space to reflect on your life goals and ambitions, the kind of thoughts and reflection your prior busy lifestyle might not have afforded you.

You'll have the opportunity to do things you don't normally have time for, to take up a new hobby, or learn new skills – such as how to speak a foreign language or become a certified scuba diver. It's important to keep learning, or have a project on the go whilst you're travelling – it's not a case of finding a way to fill your days, but your trip will be all the richer for the time spent broadening your mind, skillset, or making personal achievements along the way: whether it's simply reading more books, challenging yourself to become a better photographer, keeping a travel blog, learning a local traditional or cultural art form such as dance, yoga, martial arts, or a musical instrument, it will give a greater sense of purpose to your trip. Experiences become more valuable than possessions; just as time is more desirable than wealth. It makes the down time more rewarding and helps to make the travel lifestyle feel more sustainable.

When you come home be prepared to have a new outlook on life, and different wants and needs, and you might feel you've moved on in many ways. It's more than just a desire to hit the road again, or not wanting to go back to work (save for the need to earn money); it's personal growth, your life enriched from the experience, the culture, the people, the vistas, the good times and the bad. Your new outlook might extend to living more in the moment, quitting doing things you don't enjoy and cutting back on making extravagant or expensive purchases.

The following quote from novelist Terry Pratchett sums it up eloquently:

> "Why do you go away? So that you can come back. So that you can see the place you came from with new eyes and extra colours. And the people there see you differently, too. Coming back to where you started is not the same as never leaving."
>
> (Terry Pratchett, *A Hat Full of Sky*, published by Corgi Children's, 5th May 2005)

Without getting too spiritual about it, the most life-changing aspect is the realisation that long-term travel is accessible to everyone with a bit of forward planning. Once you've shifted your mind set and travel plans away from taking short holidays that fit into your company's annual leave policy, it's about finding a way to fit your work and lifestyle around your travel aspirations – whether it's by working remotely, taking a job abroad, or travelling between jobs, there is a multitude of ways of making travel possible and to start living the dream.

A newfound appreciation of the mundane...

The decision to go home will, all things going to plan, be a decision as opposed to a necessity – whether that means your bank account needs replenishing or you just fancy settling back into home life again. Whilst there may be many things you miss about your life on the road, there are also many things to look forward to about going home. Here are some of my favourites:

– Not having to slather on the lotions and potions

In the tropics it's thirty plus degrees by day and not much cooler by night. This means two things – you can't go out in the day without slathering on the sunscreen, or by night without the mosquito repellent.

It's humid, you sweat, and your skin is permanently greasy with the creams and sprays, sticky from the salt from swimming in the sea, and a little bit of you longs for a temperate climate, where you can leave the house bare-skinned and without sweating the minute you set foot outside the front door. Once back at home you can not only hold off on the creams and lotions, you also have the joys of a hot shower once more.

– Not living out of a bag anymore

A sixty-five-litre rucksack seems a generous enough size. As you're packing to go away, its contents are meticulously planned, listed and packed, and everything has its precise location in the bag. However, fast-forward to the fortieth time I've unpacked and repacked my bag and it's not quite so orderly – and I have to pull everything out of my bag to find the one item I'm looking for.

Oh, and why do my possessions seem to expand once I've left the country? I was sure I left home with some space to spare in my bag, but it's all I can do to stuff everything in when I'm on the move. Constantly packing and unpacking a bag really takes its toll after a while, especially if you're on the move a lot, so it's so nice to come home or even just put down roots somewhere for a while, properly unpack and not have to carry my life around on my back from one place to the next.

– Having access to all my clothes, shoes and accessories again

Airline bag size and weight restrictions means that there's space for precisely one week's worth of clothes that must be washed every week. Pack extra items for special occasions, or niche activities at your peril! You'll soon resent packing those heavy walking boots on the off chance you might climb that mountain – or the *smart* outfit in case you go somewhere posh (you probably won't, or if you do then the outfit will have to *go* with flip flops). Cue jettisoning of any non-essentials once you're on the move.

Contrast that with the feeling of arriving home and opening your wardrobe to piles of clean clothes and shoes to suit every occasion and you'll feel like you've just been on a huge shopping spree, with a newfound appreciation for your old clothes.

– Island time

I love the island lifestyle, but the lack of structured timekeeping can sometimes drive me crazy! Things happen when they're ready to: transportation leaves when it's full. A bus journey quoted as taking four hours in reality takes seven. Your laundry was promised to be washed and dried by five pm yesterday but is still not ready the following day. This is all par for the course.

So, I take a small pleasure in returning home to a more orderly lifestyle, regular transportation that at least attempts to leave on time (subject to strikes and leaves on the line!) and events more or less taking place at the advertised time.

– Stinks!

As much as you might try to keep everything smelling fresh, it's a constant challenge when living in a hot and humid climate and is exacerbated by having to pack damp items whilst on the move. Micro-fibre towels are one of the main offenders though I have to admit that they do save space and dry quicker than a standard towel.

Once home, you can wrap yourself in big, soft, fluffy towels and revel in being able to hang it out to dry until you use it again the following day. Rediscover the joys of sweet smelling laundry detergents and fabric softeners – and the luxury of being able to wash your clothes on a delicate setting, separating out your whites from your colours.

The joy of having your possessions around you again, a full wardrobe, sleeping in your own bed, hot showers and the chance to settle in one place again; you'll truly appreciate your home comforts when you get back.

So long as you're not travelling to run away from your problems, you'll see the world in a new light when you return home, with a newfound appreciation for the simple things, new friendships, renewed energy and ambition to invest in your career and goals.

But as nice as it is to settle for a while, you will soon begin to miss the road. Being home feels strangely like being back in a familiar place but everything feels completely different. You'll soon begin to miss your travelling lifestyle... and so you begin planning your next escape.

RESOURCES RECAP:

- **UK government foreign travel advice**
  www.gov.uk/foreign-travel-advice

- **US government foreign travel advice**
  https://travel.state.gov/content/passports/en/country.html

- **A Hat Full of Sky – Terry Pratchett**
  https://amzn.to/2OsIEts

9

TOP TIPS

Culture shock

You'll probably experience a few days of mild cultural shock when you arrive in a new country and it always surprises me how I feel it, even in seemingly comfortable or familiar places. There is no reason to fear it, however, so just get stuck in and immerse yourself in local culture – you'll be richly rewarded for it.

If you're unsure of the custom, watch others, or ask someone. Taking the time to find out the correct way of doing things shows respect and minimises your chances of causing offence. If you do make a faux pas, first apologise and then put things right. We all make mistakes and it's easy to do in a country that's very culturally different to your home country.

I remember being incredibly frustrated when waiting at passport control in Bangkok's Don Mueang airport. The queuing system was practically non-existent, and people kept pushing their way to the front, rather than waiting their turn. At least was how I saw it through my British eyes – and everyone knows how us Brits feel about queuing! So, rather than get mad at my fellow passengers for pushing in, I simply joined them and assertively made my way through the queue – we all just wanted to be on our way, after all.

Home comforts and global brands – whether it's Western-style restaurant chains serving your favourite meal, or Coca Cola and Oreo cookies – are usually available on even the remotest parts of the tourist trail, but some of the best experiences come from stepping outside your comfort zone and embracing local cultures, tastes and traditions.

So here are a few tips to help acclimatise you:

Saving face

Around the world, cultural norms and behaviours – what is considered polite or rude – and how to act varies. From hierarchical societies where age or status implies wisdom, to flat, informal cultures where old and young, rich and poor are all treated the same.

Remembering to use a formal register – or not – when talking to your superiors whilst recalling the vocabulary and grammar to string a sentence together can seem like a lot to recall at times, but it's important to get it right – or at least try to respect the rules. Just as you wouldn't walk around topless at a holy site or in a deeply religious society, how you speak, your tone and the language you use also makes an important impact.

For example, the Vietnamese are proud people and they care a lot about how they are perceived by others. The concept of *saving* or *losing face* is an important cultural tradition and should be considered in all interactions with a Vietnamese person. *Face* can be interpreted as social reputation, dignity or integrity, so if you are thought to be embarrassing yourself in front of others, you are *losing face.* Behaving dishonourably, lying, shouting or arguing in public is considered offensive because it causes you to *lose face.*

Looking back on my first visit to Vietnam, I committed a faux pas which – unbeknownst to me – caused my host to lose face: After staying three nights in a guest house in Ho Chi Minh City, my host asked me to write a review about my stay on the booking website. Having given a commendable score of eight out of ten, I marked the property down only on account there being no safe in the room and one or two other minor details. My host, however, did not take the review favourably and fired back an angry response:

"What did you have stolen?" From where she stood, there really didn't need to be a safety deposit box because there was no risk of my things going missing – whereas I was simply implying it might be an improvement that might make future guests feel more secure.

She ended her email, *"I hope I never see you again!"*

I learnt the hard way. It demonstrates how seemingly small cultural differences can cause individuals to be so greatly misunderstood – and how learning some basic social etiquette and customs can prevent clashes, embarrassments or misunderstandings on your travels.

The concept of *saving face* goes beyond just Vietnam and applies broadly across Southeast Asia. In a restaurant in Koh Chang, Thailand I asked a waiter how long my food would be after waiting over forty-five minutes. Not wanting to lose face, he told me mine was the next order, and that it would only be a few minutes – but on checking again in another fifteen minutes, it transpired the chef had still not started preparing it! I discreetly told him we were in a hurry and had to go. We quietly paid for our drinks and went on our way and no *face* was lost since the chef hadn't started cooking yet and I didn't make a scene.

Conversely, whilst dining with a French family in Brittany, France, I thought I was being polite by waiting for everyone to be served before starting to eat – until they asked me if I wasn't hungry or didn't like the food on my plate! They were amused to learn that in the UK, we wait for everyone to start eating together (and the person who is served first's food gets cold!) It was quite common across Southeast Asia for my travel partner or me to have been served and finished our meal before the other's had even come out of the kitchen – so this logic certainly makes sense from that perspective!

Most guide books will contain some information around cultural traditions and norms, but if you want to delve a little deeper the **Culture Smart! The Essential Guide to Customs & Culture** (www.culturesmartbooks.co.uk) series of books come highly recommended when it comes to learning about and understanding different countries' cultures; offering insights into behaviours, beliefs and attitudes, and practical tips on how to get the most out of your trip.

Change up how you drink your coffee

As you travel around the world, coffee-drinking customs change, so give up your daily flat white and adapt your coffee to the country you're in – especially if you're in a coffee-producing country like Italy, Colombia or Costa Rica, where even your most basic cup of coffee is likely to be of a high standard and is served without fuss or fancy ceremony.

In Vietnam and Laos, where fresh milk is often not available, coffee is served sweetened with condensed milk, in a thick, viscose layer in the bottom of your cup. In Rome, Italy, cappuccinos are reserved for the mornings and only the tourists drink them after lunch. In Paris, France, prices for a coffee can vary depending on where you sit in the café! It's cheapest standing at the bar and most expensive sitting at a table on the pavement or terrace. Perhaps the oddest coffee variation I tried was the **yin yang** in Hong Kong: a blend of half tea, half coffee served with milk – I can't say I ordered a second cup, but it was certainly interesting to try! Follow the locals' lead for a more authentic coffee experience and to keep the cost down.

*Coffee time –
Luang Prabang, Laos.*

Stay cool, drink beer!

I expect I'm not alone in my love for trying the national beers when I arrive in a new country. You can't beat that feeling when you've just arrived, dumped your bags in the hotel and headed out to catch the sunset over a cold beer.

From the local **Belikin** stout in Belize to the ubiquitous **Chang** beer in Thailand, every country has a national beer and, if you're lucky, there are several to choose between, so enjoy (in moderation, of course!) The same applies to locally made spirits and wines – drink local for the best experience!

As with the coffee, look out for local variations: **Michelada** in Mexico (made with beer, lime juice, and assorted sauces, spices, and peppers, served in a chilled, salt-rimmed glass) – is so refreshing on a hot day! In France, try a **Monaco**: lager, topped up with lemonade and a dash of grenadine

If you're on a budget, try one of the following options to keep your spending on track:

- Grab a cold can from the supermarket and take it to the beach with you (assuming the country that you're visiting permits drinking in public places). It'll cost you a tenth of the price you'd pay in a beach-side bar. I love to do this in Barcelona, Spain, as I can pick a quiet spot to sit away from the crowds whilst I watch the sun go down.

- Head for **happy hour** promotions: Most bars and restaurants in tourist destinations around the world try to lure the tourists in with happy hour

– which can vary in duration from an hour (as the name suggests) to all day – in the loosest sense of the expression.

- Backpacker towns are also renowned for their cheap drinks to sate impoverished and thirsty travellers. Hit the hostel bars and steer clear of expensive hotel bars if you want to party and stay on budget.

Please drink responsibly!

Top travel gadgets

Over multiple trips and holidays I have honed down my travel kit and now I never leave home on a big trip without the following tried and tested items in my rucksack.

PacSafe

I can highly recommend Pacsafe's range of Anti-Theft Backpack And Bag Protectors – they come in a range of sizes and are great when your accommodation doesn't provide a safe; if you need to leave your bag in luggage storage, or unattended on public transport. It's a lightweight, flexible and slash-proof cage that locks around your rucksack, securing your valuables inside. When you're not using it, it packs down into a compact case making it easy to carry.

To stop would-be thieves running off with your bag, you can use the device to attach your bag to a piece of furniture in your hotel room; to a luggage rack on public transport, or to a travel companion's bag – it's much harder for a thief to make off with two large rucksacks than one! Find out more here: **Pacsafe 85 Anti-Theft Backpack And Bag Protector** (https://amzn.to/2yncXyy) is suitable for a large, 65+ litre rucksack.

Osprey Farpoint/Fairview carry-on rucksacks

Travelling hand-luggage only? Maximise your carry-on allowance with these great forty-litre rucksacks. They're packed with handy pockets galore, a laptop compartment and internal straps to hold the contents in place, and you'll be amazed how much you can cram into these bags.

They are also really comfortable to wear; complete with waist and chest straps to hold the pack in place and to take the weight off your shoulders, making it a convenient for hiking as well as carry-on luggage.

The **Osprey Fairview 40** (https://amzn.to/2IIiJdH) is a women's fit and the **Osprey Farpoint 40** (https://amzn.to/2z1Jquf) is the men's version – both come in two sizes to cater for larger and smaller body types. They are ideal for shorter and longer trips, when you don't want the hassle of checking in bags – or you want to keep your eyes on your luggage whilst you're on the move.

Silk sleeping bag liner

Designed to keep your sleeping bag fresh, a silk sleeping bag liner has another great use as a stand-alone sleeping bag in hot countries. It's lighter than sleeping under cotton sheets and it keeps the mosquitoes off. It is also great if you find yourself cold on a long coach journey when the air conditioning is cranked right up or if your hotel accommodation is of a questionable standard!

It packs down, via a compression sack, to the size of a fist for easy storage and transportation, can be hand washed in the sink and dries quickly (https://amzn.to/2MvYZ0b).

Kindle

Do away with heavy, bulky guide books and novels and load everything you want to read onto a Kindle. It'll save you considerable weight and bag space, plus it's easy to download books on the go.

You can pick up a range of Kindles fairly cheaply and all your content is backed up online in your Amazon account. My favourite model is the **Paperwhite** (https://amzn.to/2lbEY2p), which comes with a backlight, making it perfect during insomnia in a hostel dorm, or at dusk when you want to continue reading whilst over a sundowner.

The **Kindle Fire** (https://amzn.to/2JGfr01) is also great as a budget tablet and e-reader in one. It contains all the functionality you need at the fraction of the price of some other tablets. You may find it a suitable alternative to taking a laptop away with you (depending on how much typing you need to do).

Noise-cancelling headphones

My **Bose Quiet Comfort** noise cancelling headphones (https://amzn.to/2t1kj5w) have been my saviour when travelling, cutting out the background noise on flights, buses and in noisy hotel rooms. They may be one of the most expensive items in my travel kit, but I won't go anywhere without them now.

I used them every night of a ten-day stay in Tulum, where my stay coincided with an extremely loud Mayan music festival that went on until 4 o'clock every morning – and I would literally have had no sleep without them. They are also useful to phase out screaming babies and snoring passengers on overnight flights and buses – plus they give you a better quality of listening on your headphones, so your music sounds good wherever your surroundings.

To beat insomnia, listen to **Sleep Sound** (http://bit. do/sleepsound) on your noise cancelling headphones. A soundtrack designed to help you sleep in noisy environments, Sleep Sound features calming rainfall, waves and waterfalls interwoven into a wall of soporific white noise; engineered to block out background noise whilst simultaneously coaxing you to sleep.

Laptop

My laptop is an integral part of my travel kit and I use it for keeping in touch with loved ones back home, blogging, trip research and booking the next leg of my trip. Consider getting a lightweight, slim-line netbook – your bag and your back will thank you in the long run!

It goes without saying but always back up regularly – especially any work you've done and photos you've taken along the way in case something happens to your computer. Laptops and cameras can be replaced, photos can't – and whilst you'll always have the memories, you'll cherish looking back over your pictures, so take good care of your files.

There are many Cloud storage websites out there to choose from. **Google Drive** (www.Google.com/drive), **OneDrive** (https://onedrive.live.com), **Dropbox** (www. dropbox.com) – and others – all offer free Cloud storage and are a great way of backing up important documents, files and photos whilst you're on the move, and which can be accessed from any computer via the Internet. All the above sites also have handy mobile apps, so you can access, back up and manage files from your smartphone.

If you need more storage that the free plan offers, you can purchase a monthly or annual plan but before you buy, think about spreading your files over a few free Cloud-based accounts. (Top tip: always do your backing up over a fast Wi-Fi connection, or it will take ages to upload large files like photos.)

It's also worth backing up everything onto a portable hard drive like this one: https://amzn.to/2lf8EvK – it's less valuable to a thief than a laptop, so there's less chance of it being stolen; plus, it's a way of accessing your files when you don't have Wi-Fi and can't get onto the Cloud.

Multi-country adaptor plug with USB sockets

Charge your laptop, phone and e-reader all at once with these handy multi-country adaptor plugs with USB sockets. The USB ports make light work of charging all your devices at once, and you don't have to carry around a bulky charger for every device. From your phone to your Kindle, MP3 player to portable power bank, it's charging made easy.

Amazon has a huge selection or adaptor plugs, including this one: https://amzn.to/2tfaWyn.

Portable power bank

A portable battery or power bank with enough charge to top up your phone is a life-saver for long journeys; if your phone dies when you're out and about or as an emergency power source during power cuts. I used the Anker PowerCore 5000 Portable Charger (https://amzn.to/2t9Ncvq), which is enough to fully charge your phone or MP3 player.

I also found it useful to take a portable battery charger in my travel kit to keep my torch and headphones batteries charged up – but your need will depend on how many devices you take with you.

Travel SIM card

Having access to calls, maps and email will be a life-saver at times – if you're wandering around trying to find your accommodation, unable to locate it with the directions given, you can simply call them.

Before you set off, make sure your phone is unlocked and check with your mobile phone service provider to see if roaming in the countries you intend to visit is included in your tariff. If it isn't, remember to turn off the data roaming on your phone when you arrive – or you could end up with an exorbitant phone bill that you haven't budgeted for! Then pick up a local SIM card when you land – remember you'll need your passport in order to get a SIM, so don't forget to take it with you to the phone shop.

My top travel apps

Once you've packed your travel bags, download the following useful apps onto your phone to keep you on track whilst you're on the move.

Galileo

Picture the scene: you've just arrived off a long flight and successfully navigated the public transport/taxi to the area where you'll be staying. But now the taxi driver isn't exactly sure where your place is – and you forgot to print off a paper map.

This is where Galileo steps in, offering free offline maps – no roaming required. Just download the country map over Wi-Fi before you travel, and you'll have access to them without needing to use any data on your phone.

The free version is great, but for a nominal fee, upgrade to the *Pro* version which gives you access to an offline search function, the ability to drop pins and add bookmarks. I have used this app on every trip and couldn't go away without it now.

Visit https://galileo-app.com/ for more details.

Caxton FX

Caxton FX (www.caxtonfx.com) is a pre-paid credit card which permits you to load the ten most popular currencies (including GBP, US dollars and euros) onto a MasterCard for use as a debit card whilst you are abroad. There are no foreign transaction fees and no fees for using ATMs abroad.

You can withdraw cash in any currency (even if you have a different currency loaded onto your card, Caxton will convert it for you), so if your intended destination's currency is not available to load, just load British pounds, euros, or US dollars. You can also load your card when the exchange rate is favourable, and lock in that rate.

The Caxton FX app is really easy to use and it takes seconds to load money onto your card. Protect your travel funds by loading on a small amount at a time (£100 minimum load) so you don't have to worry about taking your bank debit or credit cards out with you.

Curve

To make a foreign currency transaction on your credit card without any associated foreign transaction fees, **Curve Card** converts the transaction at near-perfect market rates and transfers it onto your credit card with no foreign exchange fee (most foreign transactions on a credit card come with a 3% fee).

Simply link your Curve card to your chosen Visa or MasterCard credit or debit card and keep track of all your transactions via the simple-to-use app. You can also block your card via the app if it gets lost or stolen (and unblock it if you find it again!)

The benefits of Curve mean you can continue to spend on existing debit or credit cards, without needing to apply for a new travel credit card. Linking to existing credit cards also means you continue to earn reward points from your credit card as every transaction that goes through Curve is simply transferred as a purchase to your credit card account.

Find out more at www.imaginecurve.com and use the promotional code KWZEV when you apply for £5 credit on your first transaction.

Booking.com

With great search and filter functionality, www.booking.com is my one-stop-shop for accommodation when I'm travelling. Whether you're making reservations months in advance or very last minute, **Booking.com** offers competitive rates and a wide range of accommodation options from hostels and guesthouses to hotel chains and high-end, luxury resorts.

You can filter search results by facilities, area, price, customer review score and more, so it's easy to find the best accommodation for your needs.

Cross reference search results against **TripAdvisor** (www.tripadvisor.com) for candid traveller reviews and for recommendations for nearby restaurants and activities – which are great when you've just arrived somewhere, and you don't know the area yet.

It's easy to cancel and amend bookings, or to ask your host questions via the app.

Before you book, however, it is worth shopping around – compare prices for the same hotels via different travel booking sites. **Expedia** (www.expedia.co.uk), **Hotels.com** (https://uk.hotels.com), **Hostelworld** (www.hostelworld.com), **Trivago** (www.trivago.co.uk), **Kayak** (www.kayak.co.uk) – and others – often have the same rooms for sale at different prices. Some will have availability where others do not, so research the best deal before booking.

Tripit

Consolidate and save all your travel plans to view offline in this easy-to-use app. Simply set up your free account then email your booking confirmations to plans@tripit.com and **Tripit** will save down all the details to a consolidated itinerary. You can save details of flights, hotels, ground transportation, ferries, tours, activities and more, with Tripit converting the booking details in the email into their user interface with minimum effort on your part. Then add your fellow travellers to your itinerary so they can access the same details and add plans too.

For a monthly charge, you can upgrade to the Pro version and Tripit will send you updates with gate information at the airport, track frequent flyer balances and more – but I would recommend trying the free version first before shelling out. Find out more at www.tripit.com

WiFiMap

Never be stuck without Wi-Fi again! **WiFiMap** (www. wifimap.io) is a user-updated database containing over one hundred million accessible Wi-Fi hotspot locations and passwords. Wherever you are in the world, simply open the app to access the passwords of nearby networks. When you've connected to a new network, you can also update the database for other users. The only catch is that you need to be online to connect and download the database. Upgrade to the pro version for a one-off charge and download an entire city's Wi-Fi passwords before you get there so you can access them offline when you arrive.

XE.com

Keep on top of exchange rates as you hop from country to country. Simply download the **XE.com** (https://xe.com) app, add in the currencies you want to track and turn your phone into a portable exchange rate calculator. Whether you've just arrived in a country and are not sure what the local currency is worth, or you need to do a quick spot check to make sure you're not about to be scammed, XE.com will keep you up to date and can even be used offline once you have added your currencies to the list.

Speedtest.net

Speedtest.net (www.speedtest.net) is an invaluable resource on the road: a website which enables you to run an internet speed test – testing upload and download speeds in a short thirty-second test.

On my recent travels, if I had work to do or calls to make and needed a fast connection, I would ask the host to run the test remotely before booking online or do it in person on arrival – before handing over the money for the accommodation.

The **SimpleSpeed** app for iPhone offers the same functionality in an app for convenience on the go.

Simple Speed Test screenshot – there's decent WiFi here!

Award Wallet

Do you find it hard to remember all your loyalty and frequent flyer account login details; lose track of balances and the expiry date of points? Then let **Award Wallet** (www.awardwallet.com) do it for you. Create an account, enter all your reward account details and Award Wallet will monitor your balances, notify you about movements in your accounts and send you an alert when the points are due to expire.

Keeping track of your balances also helps safeguard against *Loyalty Fraud*, where hackers gain unauthorised access to your loyalty accounts and steal your points. By staying aware of current balances, you can quickly take action with the loyalty account provider if you notice any suspicious activity in your account.

RESOURCES RECAP:

- **Culture Smart books** www.culturesmart.co.uk
- **Pacsafe 85 Anti-Theft Backpack And Bag Protector** https://amzn.to/2yncXyy
- **Osprey Fairview 40** https://amzn.to/2IIiJdH
- **Osprey Farpoint 40** https://amzn.to/2z1Jquf
- **Silk sleeping bag liner** https://amzn.to/2MvYZ0b
- **Kindle Paperwhite** https://amzn.to/2lbEY2p
- **Kindle Fire** https://amzn.to/2JGfr01
- **Bose Quiet Comfort headphones** https://amzn.to/2t1kj5w

- **Sleep Sound** http://bit.do/sleepsound
- **Google Drive** www.Google.com/drive
- **OneDrive** https://onedrive.live.com
- **Dropbox** www.dropbox.com
- **External hard drive** https://amzn.to/2lf8EvK
- **Adaptor plug with USB sockets** https://amzn.to/2tfaWyn
- **Power bank** https://amzn.to/2t9Ncvq
- **Galileo** https://galileo-app.com/
- **Caxton FX** www.caxtonfx.com
- **Curve card** www.imaginecurve.com
- **Booking.com** www.booking.com
- **TripAdvisor** www.tripadvisor.com
- **Expedia** www.expedia.co.uk
- **Hotels.com** https://uk.hotels.com
- **Hostelworld** www.hostelworld.com
- **Trivago** www.trivago.co.uk
- **Kayak** www.kayak.co.uk
- **Tripit** www.tripit.com
- **WifiMap** www.wifimap.io
- **XE.com** www.xe.com
- **Speedtest.net** www.speedtest.net
- **Award Wallet** www.awardwallet.com

THANK YOU

Thank you for reading – I hope you have found some inspiration to break the holiday mould and plan for a longer trip, be it in one, five or ten years' time!

I hope you now realise that anyone – even you! – can make long-term travel a reality if you really want to. Good luck!

For more information, please visit www.admin.land/travel-secret, where you will also find a list of all links contained in this book.

Thank you to all contributors; to Kevin Kerrigan for his support; to Sarah Houldcroft for the publishing; to Helen Lopez for legal advice; and to Becky Kummer, Gary Macauley, Tim Fleischman, Siobhan Lavin, Lindsay Taylor and Zoe Wiggins for proofreading and feedback along the way.

ABOUT THE AUTHOR

Sarah lives with her husband in London, UK and her favourite pastimes are bungee jumping, flying trapeze, red wine and fine dining – though obviously not all at the same time!

When she's not travelling around the world, Sarah works as an Executive Assistant and runs her own Virtual Assistant business, www.admin.land.

Sarah has completed two extended trips to date, and her third, to South America, is next on the cards.

Having enjoyed writing blogs to keep friends and family up to date whilst she travels, Sarah decided to take it to the next level by writing this book, to share her tips, stories and experience.

You can follow her book-writing adventures and get in touch by visiting www.admin.land/travel-secret.

NOTE PAGES FOR YOUR BIG TRIP

....
....
....
....
....
....
....
....
....
....
....
....
....
....
....
....
....

....

....

....

....

....

....

....

....

....

....

....

....

....

....

....

....

Printed in Great Britain
by Amazon